Bobby Charlton's
BOOK OF
EUROPEAN
FOOTBALL

Number 4

BOBBY CHARLTON'S BOOK
of EUROPEAN FOOTBALL
Number 4

Forewords by Gordon Banks, and Terry Hennessey

THE STAR LINE-UP

BILLY BREMNER   FRANK O'FARRELL

MALCOLM MUSGROVE   TED MACAULEY   RALPH COATES   WIM VAN HANEGEM

GEORGE EASTHAM   ALEXANDRE BAPTISTA

SOUVENIR PRESS LTD • *LONDON*

First published 1972 by Souvenir Press Ltd., 95 Mortimer
Street, London, W.1, and simultaneously in Canada by
J. M. Dent & Son (Canada) Ltd., Ontario, Canada.

ISBN 0 285 62052 5

Printed in Great Britain by
Gilmour & Dean Ltd., Hamilton and London

CONTENTS

Dave Mackay in his last season at Derby.

List of Illustrations

LIST OF ILLUSTRATIONS—*continued*

Gordon Banks . . .
the great goalkeeper of
our generation.

Bobby —my old pal..

— FOREWORD —
By GORDON BANKS
STOKE CITY & ENGLAND

MY earliest recollections of Bobby Charlton were painful ones. We were only kids, probably around 17 or 18, playing in the Northern Intermediate Youth Cup Final.

I was in goal for Chesterfield and Bobby was playing inside forward for Manchester United's youth side. He was in and out of the senior side then but was still entitled to play for the youngsters.

I had heard all about him and I had read about his fantastic skill and shooting ability—but I found out for myself first hand when we met for the first of two legs at Old Trafford.

He peppered my goal with such power that my hands were still smarting an hour after the game. I can't remember whether he scored; but he certainly gave me cause to remember his shooting prowess. We lost the final 4–3.

I have been impressed ever since by the awesome power of his shot, probably the hardest I have ever faced from anybody anywhere in the world of soccer. It's both fortunate—for me— and unfortunate—for the fans—that he doesn't play in positions now which give him more chance to shoot.

As a man there's none finer. He is probably the most modest star, in any profession, that you could ever meet. Even when he gained his 100th England cap, and scored too, as if to celebrate it himself, he was almost petrified with embarrassment about it all, about all the fuss.

I congratulated him on his magnificent achievement: and I must say I felt just as big a thrill for him as he probably did for himself. He was simply too modest to make any show about it. It might have been the first time for all he was concerned. But underneath I know he was tingling with pride.

Over the years I have feared and respected him as an opponent—and have grown to enjoy his company as a man outside the game.

Terry Hennessey.

Bobby —my old idol!

FOREWORD
By TERRY HENNESSEY
DERBY COUNTY & WALES

WHAT can you say about this man Bobby Charlton? It's enough to say that he must be the perfect model for any youngster setting out on a football career.

People will look at my vanishing hairline—just like Bobby's—and scoff when I say I used to watch him play for Manchester United when I was a schoolboy!

I used to trek from Wrexham, North Wales, where I was born and where I was living when Bobby got into United's first team. I was playing for the Welsh schoolboy eleven and was mad keen, quite naturally, on the game.

He was an outside left then with tremendous pace, power of shot, acceleration and with a body swerve that would fool any defender into error.

If he was great then he became even greater when he moved inside and into midfield. The involvement seemed to add more to his game; he became a superb passer of the ball and able to loft it 40 and 50 yards, accurately and apparently without any effort.

I suppose I have been matched against him four or five times at international level and he has always been the fairest of players, honest in his approach to the game and full of enthusiasm for it and for England.

I have also felt the impact of one or two of his shots and I can tell you they hurt!

But it's not only his soccer skills that fill me with respect for him. His attitude to all and sundry, humble or important, is precisely the same, one of gentlemanliness.

He's a top class sportsman—and the sort of competitor that every side hopes to have in its ranks.

It's a shame for England that he cannot go on for ever. They have found nobody yet to replace him.

Kiddo and the

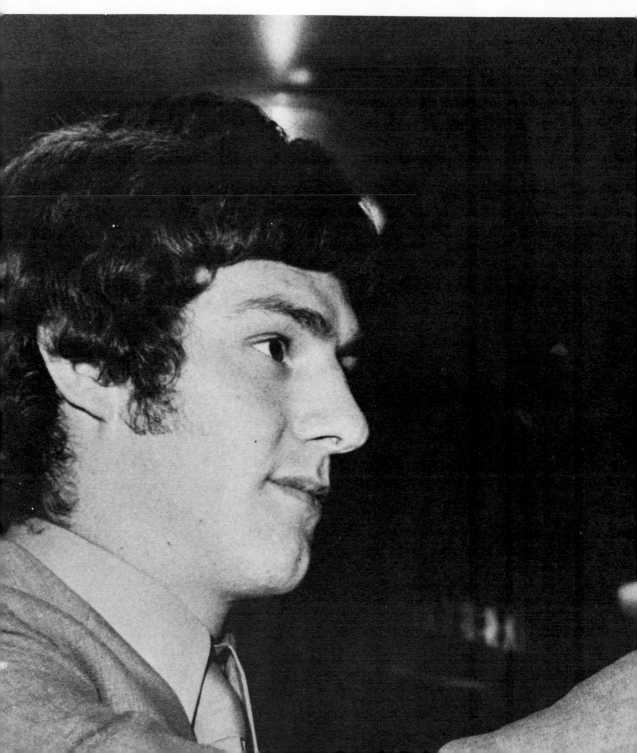

Kidder

Brian Kidd of Manchester United, 'Kiddo' to the Stretford End fans, and the big fight game's No. 1 kidder, Muhammed Ali. They got together in Manchester when Muhammed former world heavyweight champion was on a tour of this country last year.

THE JET

SET STA

TED MACAULEY, describes a fabulous private jet flight into Europe with Bobby Charlton to see budding international footballers proudly showing their mettle under the auspices of a great Ford of Europe competition for soccer kids.

DATELINE FARO . . . Bobby walks to his executive jet for the start of his tour.

BOBBY CHARLTON'S flight of fancy to meet the top soccer kids of Europe and Malta lifted him and me into the high flying world of millionaire style living.

I joined the jet-setters for a fabulous trip across the face of Europe in a £500,000 Hawker Siddeley 125, nine seats of luxury class in Ford's executive aircraft.

Bobby had joined forces with Ford of Europe to help promote a programme of football skills among continental youngsters—and his main job was to be present at the finals in each country to encourage the lads and give away the prizes to the successful soccer kids.

The programme has been an enormous success, undertaken with smooth efficiency and attractive enough to have boys in their thousands flooding the company's local representatives with entries.

In fact, more than 25,000 boys took part in the programme during 1971—which, in itself, presents a frightening organisational problem.

Briefly, the boys have to undergo various tests of skill and points are awarded according to their merit; the tests take in as many aspects of the basics as possible, shooting, passing, running, heading and general fitness.

They were, however, difficult enough to keep Bobby from having a go himself in case he made a mess of it all!

As he said: "I'd feel an awful fool if, for instance, I had a go at the penalty test and failed it when some of these little fellows are whacking the ball home with such great accuracy.

"I've kept my appearances purely formal on these occasions with no joining in. In fact, at one contest in Strasbourg somebody threw a ball to me and, instinctively, I caught it on my instep and brought it down okay. And I thought:

DATELINE VALE DU LOBO: With wife Norma and family.

'Thank the Lord that came off all right'."

"I'd have looked daft if it hadn't. So I decided there and then not to get any more involved than that."

Bobby, such a force in world football and a model for any aspiring soccer youngster was a natural choice as the player to represent the Ford company. His own enthusiasm, his tremendous interest in children, his authority and his reputation as a man of fair play, honesty and unforgettable skill at his own game, made him the absolute ideal for a job of this nature.

When he was asked he readily agreed to do the job, even though it meant giving up a lot of his spare time, often necessitating long, arduous journeys right after a match in England to get to far flung soccer outposts. This is a side of Bobby's life that few people in Britain realised existed.

It even invaded the only real good holiday break he had had for years in 1971—but he willingly sacrificed a slice out of his vacation in Portugal to fly off for four days of travel to meet Europe's soccer kids.

And that's when I joined up with him for a tiring but unforgettable long weekend of almost non-stop air travel, more travel by car, overnights at luxury hotels, and fun with Charlton, a man with a highly developed sense of humour, wittier than his sometimes sombre countenance will allow him credit for.

Indeed, when the journey was at its most tiring, when yawns were coming far too easily and the body was starting to ache with fatigue, even in luxury class surroundings, it was Bobby's light-heartedness, despite his dislike for flying, that pulled us all back to brightness.

It all started at Stansted Airport, Essex, where Ford have their private squadron of aircraft under the command of Captain John Wilson, a former airline pilot with such built-in competance that any misgivings one might have about flying appear utterly ludicrous in this man's comforting presence.

Bobby, along with his wife, Norma, and their two daughters were holidaying at Vale du Lobo on the Algarve in Portugal and Fords were sending their executive jet, and crew of three, to collect him.

I joined Captain Wilson, hostess Paddy Farmer, and Fordmen Joe Vick, the then organiser of the contest, and John Goffin, who later took over from Mr. Vick.

The nose of the sleek silver and blue liveried jet thrust through the rain clouds around Essex, turned south towards Portugal and settled at 40,000-feet and 600 miles an hour for the three-hour journey to the sunshine of Faro.

Over Paris . . . the Pyrenees . . . across Spain and Portugal until the wide arc of the area around Faro, the incredible blue sea and the bronze sands, could be seen stretched out far below us.

Bobby was already down there, sunning himself after the rigours of a season of English soccer campaigning, as the Ford jet swooped out of the shimmering haze to land at Faro airport, a place so hot in the June heat as to take your breath away.

Then, like a private cab, the 'plane waited overnight while we drove to collect Bobby from his holiday hotel.

The day after Norma and the children kissed Bobby goodbye as the England international set off to work, his coat slung over his shoulder, a briefcase in hand.

We motored past the donkey carts, the scorched looking land, stucco cottages and the black-hatted farmers and back to the jet at Faro.

The second leg of the journey was to Zurich, the German speaking section of Switzerland where Bobby was to officiate at a final to be held in the Zurich Grasshoppers stadium on the fringe of the city.

But first we stopped off for a meal at the superb Hilton Hotel, close by the airport. It was, indeed, luxury all the way. Only now the heat was more oppressive than it had been in Portugal; the city humidity was uncomfortable, but it did nothing to dampen the enthusiasm of the boys in the contest. They were all far too anxious to show Bobby what they could do to allow any discomfort to put them off their stride.

16

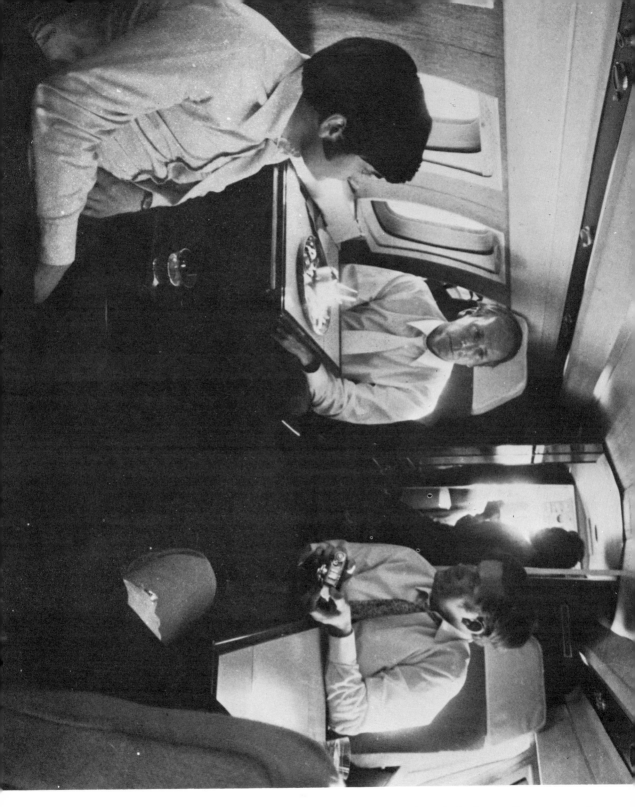

DATELINE STRATOSPHERE: Bobby and associates in business talks at 40,000 ft.

Bobby, stripped off his jacket, circled the boys as they sweated through their tests giving encouragement and, finally, presenting them with their hard-earned prizes and trophies.

They were all still cheering as we left on the third leg of Bobby's flight of fancy—this time, after a car ride back to Zurich airport and with a short stay in the VIP lounge, the next stop was Amsterdam, Holland's beautiful capital.

Even as we were hurtling along the runway the weather, so threatening all day, broke and the black clouds gave out with the thunder they had promised. . .

A big Swissair jet, bound for America, was allowed to turn away from the biggest mass of black cloud but we, being a smaller, swifter 'plane, were told by air traffic control to go through it to our flight level.

For our comfort Captain Wilson had argued the point with the Swiss controllers—but it made no difference and through it we went with enough lurching to keep us on the edge of our seats until we got to clear air.

The next leg of the journey was only 90 minutes and Captain Wilson, bringing the absolute touch calmness and consideration into his duties, said expansively: "Gentlemen, if it gets too bumpy let me know and I'll find a way round it for you." How's that for service?

Amsterdam, twinkling down below, was our next stop; three countries in one day. We hardly knew where we were or what language we would hear next.

Schiphol airport felt smooth under the wheels of the jet as we touched down like some millionaire group arriving with eye-catching splendour.

We were scheduled to make an overnight stop in the city and we spent the time at a plush hotel that formed the join of five of Holland's famous canals, a really idyllic place.

The following day, Sunday, Bobby was driven for a long day's work among the Dutch kids at a magnificently appointed sports centre at Zyst, a small town some 40 miles from Amsterdam.

The place, set in woodland, was a paradise for sportsminded youngsters and their parents. It

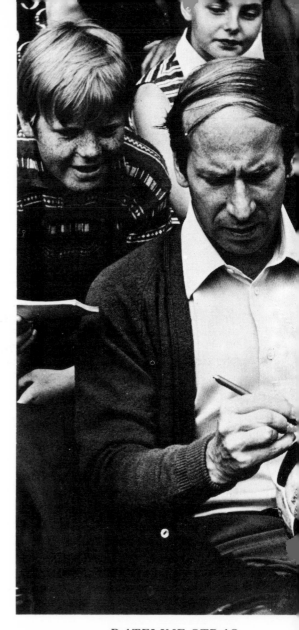

DATELINE STRAS-BOURG: Boys are boys the world over. One waits anxiously at my back as I autograph a ball.

had just about everything one could wish for. Super playing fields, practice grounds, an excellent cafe and all the trappings of a well thought out plan formulated solely for the promotion of sport and fitness.

Bobby, as usual, vanished into a vast crowd of well-wishers almost at every stride and we were constantly having to rescue him so he could carry on with the rest of the programme without being thrown off his time-table.

Even though we were in the third country in a day the boys could all have been the same nationality, their common link was the undisguised looks of admiration they gave Bobby wherever he went, the way they followed him like a soccer Pied Piper.

I cannot imagine another footballer in the world having such an effect. Plainly, he was their hero—and he made sure they got a good look at him. He signed countless autographs and posed happily for hundreds of photographs taken by proud parents who shoved their boys by Bobby's side to be pictured with the great man.

After the memorable day at Zyst we made a dash back to Schiphol airport for the long return leg to far-away Faro where Bobby could resume the holiday rest he had broken.

We had dinner at 40,000 feet—but even then, even with the tour over, Bobby's work wasn't finished. He signed hundreds of photographs of himself that were to be used as prizes . . . eating with one hand, autographing with the other.

At Faro, the Algarve's airport, which is normally closed at night, the control staff had stayed on duty to guide in the luxury jet. It was turned midnight but they were delighted to keep the place open for their VIP guest.

The whirlwind weekend was over for Bobby and he set off for his hotel, loaded with presents for his daughters, flowers for his wife, with the happy smile of a man who knew, without saying, or without being told, that he had done a satisfactory job.

As Bobby's taxi set out down the winding road towards his sea edge hotel at Vale du Lobo we stretched our legs in the early-hours warmth of the Faro tarmac waiting for the HS 125 to be re-fuelled.

And away we went for a dawn landing at Stansted, with the rain slanting grey and cold from the heavens and we knew we were home again.

It had all seemed like a dream world, one we had briefly shared with people who lived like that all the time—people like film stars Richard Burton and Liz Taylor, Henry Ford himself and the Sinatra's of this life who all have their own private jets.

We could look back on the breathtaking log of stylish living, with tycoon treatment included at every stop, that went like this. . .

Stansted Airport to Faro, 1075 miles in three hours five minutes; Faro to Zurich, 1071 miles in two hours 50 minutes: Zurich to Amsterdam, 450 miles in one and a half hours: Amsterdam to Faro, 1520 miles in three hours 25 minutes: Faro to Stansted, 1075 miles in three hours. Nearly 5200 miles! Almost the distance to America and back again on an exhausting goodwill mission to promote the world's finest game.

High over Switzerland Bobby, sipping a brandy, talked about the programme. . .

He said: "I know this job takes up quite a bit of my spare time and it has even broken into my holiday, the best break I've had for years, but I enjoy it.

"I enjoy getting out among the kids who are plainly so keen on football.

"Soccer has given me a great life and if these kids are keen enough to want to follow on then it is up to people like me to give them as much help and encouragement as I can.

"This is where Fords are doing a great job. They're a big company with big ideas and go-ahead schemes and they have hit on a truly great idea with this soccer programme.

"They have managed to project it with an admirable formula that seems to have hit the nail on the head.

"You have only to look at the expressions on the boys' faces to see how much they are enjoying it all, to see how much effort they are prepared to

DATELINE HOLLAND : And a trio of champions show off their trophies.

put into the game and its testing complexities.

"It's a pity really that there is no parallel plan at home in Britain. I'm sure it would go down as well, if not better, than it does in Europe.

"Imagine all those kids in Liverpool or in Manchester, with their great enthusiasm, given an outlet for their skills where they can win individual prizes and get recognition for their talent on their own merit.

"It seems a shame that the very place where soccer began is not served by a scheme to match that which Ford have organised in Europe. If there were I'd be happy to support it and help out as much as I could and that goes, I am sure, for many other professional players in Britain."

Fordman John Goffin, who followed master-minder Joe Vick into the soccer programme, expanded Bobby's coverage down as far as Malta and whisked him off there straight after the Manchester United versus Leicester City game at Old Trafford.

John laid on another private 'plane and, with

Ford chiefs from all over Europe, flew to Malta, a stronghold of Manchester United support.

He looked round the arena peppered with running, jumping, wriggling, writhing young-sters, all with a ball at their feet, and said: "The response to this contest is, at times, unbelievable. And it is going to get even bigger.

"Bobby has worked terribly hard to make it a success—and he's been a revelation to work with, a fine ambassador for the sport generally but for English soccer particularly.

"There are many men who simply wouldn't have bothered themselves, who would have been difficult to deal with, but even as important and famous as he is Bobby has been as keen as any of us."

I personally have rarely seen such tremendous enthusiasm among boys and, more important, in such vast numbers. Their goal, I suppose, was to look good while Bobby was watching and they certainly tried hard enough.

LEE..
ONE PEN!

. . . and another step toward his season's record. The keeper moving left to the Lee penalty going right is Peter Shilton of Leicester City.

FIVE IN A LINE.

AND A TURN-UP FOR THE BOOK

It happened in a Coventry City–Manchester United match at Old Trafford in the 1971–72 season. These five Coventry City players refused to move ten yards off the ball and the referee booked the lot of them.

I take charge of the aristocrats

MALCOLM MUSGROVE, Manchester United's soccer intellectual, is a persuasive talker and a coach of extraordinary perception. Here he tells the background story to a great club and its super stars.

MANCHESTER UNITED'S rightful heritage is a place among the world's football aristocrats and when you are given a job like mine to do with a club so great there is a feeling of pride at being at the heart of the splendour of it all.

When Frank O'Farrell was offered the job of managing United in succession to Sir Matt Busby he telephoned me and asked me to join his set-up at Old Trafford.

The enormity of the challenge intrigued me— but never scared me. The playing staff fascinated me and the chance to help to remould them for Europe's bigger glories was too much of an attractive proposition to turn down.

I could, just about then, have got a position as a manager of my own team but the thought of stepping into the atmosphere of Old Trafford, with all its splendid traditions, proved to be a greater magnet.

The aura of Manchester United is so great as to cloud any other priorities and that's a feeling which runs throughout the club, from the manager, the players the coaching staff and down, I am sure, to the gatemen.

I am only human and, like anybody else faced with such a challenge, I had my apprehensions. I had no doubt about my own ability to be able to coach and inject new ideas but I wondered whether I could get it over to the players without sparking any feeling of resentment.

After all I was going to be dealing with players of world-class stature; men almost as big as the game itself.

In my mind's eye I ranged the spectrum of players I would be handling; Bobby Charlton, George Best, Denis Law, Brian Kidd, Willie Morgan, David Sadler, Alex Stepney, all men who were virtually priceless and who had all tasted the grand rewards of football with Manchester United.

I didn't know them personally. I had met some of them during my playing days with West Ham and, of course, I knew them all by reputation.

"Bobby was
trying to
do everything
for Manchester
United, and it
wasn't
humanly
possible for
him to accept
and survive"

But what made them tick, what motivated them and their skills was a mystery to me, something to be discovered.

The enjoyment, in the first part, was going to be in discovery. And it was going to be a hard time, too.

All the worst kinds of rumours had filtered through to me before I took up the appointment and some more even while I was setting myself up in Manchester. There was, naturally, some truth in some of them—but for the most part they were largely hearsay that didn't trouble my mind.

I had heard that Denis Law was difficult to handle, that he wasn't fit, didn't believe in himself any more and that he had been finished for two years.

I had heard, too, that Willie Morgan could only run the line as a winger. That he was lazy, a coward and couldn't be bothered to get involved in the game or go looking for the ball when it wasn't played right to him.

George Best, of course, came into it. Time after time I was told he was too temperamental, too big-headed and wouldn't knuckle down to orders; that he lived a life far too wild for a footballer and that he was always late for training and sometimes didn't bother to turn up at all.

He was, I was informed, petulant and arrogant and argued too often with officials. Brian Kidd didn't escape criticism either. . .

I heard that he, too, was a petulant youngster, too big for his boots. A glory seeker without much regard for those playing around him in the same team.

There is no smoke without fire and, in part, there was basis to some of these views expressed frequently to me in all areas of football interest. But I refused to allow any of it to concern me. I could only find out for myself. And I was agreeably surprised.

Before the season opened I moved into my office at Old Trafford, just along the corridor, from the boss's and waited for all the "petulance", all the "arrogance" and all the "difficulties" to come flowing in. They didn't. . . .

I met the players almost one by one as they turned up for the new season. And, over three days, I'd met the complete playing staff with one or two exceptions, fellows who were still away on holiday. Bobby Charlton, for instance, was still away having a long needed break and he was one of the last men I met.

I knew, even on these first meetings, that I was dealing with an outfit of complete professionals, men who knew their job, stars who needed no teaching, who wanted only direction. And I resolved then to make that my ploy. It paid off, I think.

One by one I began to list what can only be described as their failings and set about making adjustments within the framework of the team as a unit without impairing their natural ability to improvise and still reveal their character as individual performers.

I thought Brian Kidd must be mad. There he was at 21 wanting to leave Manchester United, the greatest club in the world because, he said, his face didn't fit. He may have been going through a bad time and he may have suffered one or two disappointments but I knew that he couldn't really and truly want to leave Old Trafford.

At 21 he had tasted the sweetest delicacies of soccer rewards; he had experienced more at his young age than ten other professionals of twice his age had done. And, it seemed to me, he wanted to be a star without completing his apprenticeship.

I think Brian, of all the players there, has benefited more and is a better player now than before Frank O'Farrell and I took over.

He has developed a greater feeling of responsibility and accepted what I told him and the rest of the players: "Don't go looking for glory otherwise it will pass you by. Let it come, work for it."

Brian seemed content if he scored a goal and did nothing else in a game—but not any more. Now he plays wider, pulls defenders towards him on the flank and allows our other front runners to get in.

I remember at one early game where he got

Brian Kidd, eye steadily on ball, beat off this challenge.

whacked and went down groaning and moaning. I ran on with the sponge and he said: "Mal, I'll have to come off."

He'd been having a great game and I think he may have seen himself as the limping hero being cheered all the way to glory by the fans.

I told him: "Don't be daft. Are you a man or a mouse? What's the matter with you? If I were playing as well as you I'd stay on until the lights fused."

He got up again, stamped his foot once or twice to test his leg, and finished up with a rip-roaring performance. And I've never had any trouble from him since. Now you'd have to drag him off.

Denis Law has to believe he's fit and anything less than 100 percent is, for him, just not good enough. His sort of style demands strength of running, not for hundreds of yards but for quick sprints of 20 or 30 yards.

He took a kick at Old Trafford when we were playing Leicester and he wanted to come off; he's stopped believing in himself. There was only ten minutes to go to half-time so we made him stay on—and he scored a cracker which needed all of his quick-stepping agility.

But, during the interval, he asked again if he could quit and we sent him back for another short second half spell to keep Leicester unsettled if nothing else. Well, he followed up a shot from Bobby Charlton that Peter Shilton let go, only for an instant, but there was Denis right on him and the ball was in the net before Shilton could realise what was happening.

Then we pulled him off the park; his injury wasn't the sort that could be aggravated and it did him no harm but he wasn't happy because he didn't feel that 100 percent fitness.

Denis is a fantastic trainer, a quiet man off the field, who really works hard at getting himself right on the top line of fitness. That's his keyword.

Few people know it but when Denis can't train because of some injury or other he gets himself off to a gym and murders himself with weights. He refuses to shirk work that will keep on the peak of fitness.

He certainly is not a difficult man to handle. Far from it—he's the model professional, a tremendous competitor. He's an entertainer and a great character and when he looks as if he's arguing with the referee and the linesmen he's usually doing it in the best of spirits.

We don't like the players disputing decisions with the referee and we have tried to instill this feeling into the lads. We'd rather have them walk away from trouble because argument only upsets concentration. The opposition teams are trying hard enough to do that without enlisting the aid of the officials to do it as well.

My feelings are that most teams are hard enough to beat when we have eleven men on the field; to have one sent off for arguing, or for anything for that matter, throws a whole lot of weight on the remaining ten men.

There is no bravado in it, nothing gained except a seat on the bench and the frustration of knowing you have let the team down.

This is where George Best has matured a lot. He was constantly at odds with the referees and the linesmen a couple of years ago and it got him nowhere. Then, when he was sent off at Chelsea at the start of the 1971–72 season, just for passing a remark, I think he realised the futility of it all.

Ironically, that sending off seemed to develop the character of the team. They came out again without George in the second half and still managed to score a great victory 3–2. They fought like demons without George and shared the workload with sincere appreciation of each other's problems.

When we were travelling home later that evening I had a long talk with George about his role with United and asked him where he liked to play.

He told me: "Right up front. Striker."

And I said: "Do you mean second striker, picking up the ball from somebody else?"

"No," replied George", I mean right in the thick of it all. The front man."

Because of his tremendous mobility, his screening of the ball and his killing shot with either foot, that's where we put him.

FIRST
STEP
TO
STARDOM

One of the great moments of any young player's life . . . his first goal in the big League. And it came for Sammy McIlroy of Manchester United last season like this in a game against Manchester City. George Best has let the ball run on to him. Tony Book, centre, has seen the danger too late, and McIlroy has shot the goal which gave United a win.

He's so brave that I wonder about him. He takes more punishment than ten other men and comes up, usually, without moaning. If you saw his legs after some games you'd be horrified.

But he bounces right back. He's such an amazing fellow and his recovery rate is incredible.

At the start of the season he had a terrible injury to his left foot. He couldn't, at times, even get his boot on and for ten weeks he played almost on one leg but still shirking nothing, however strong the tackle or hard the challenge.

He didn't make a public issue of it and I think very few people outside Old Trafford knew just what was wrong. But that's a testimony of George's great strength of mind and willingness to accept injury without grumbling.

George doesn't have a great deal to say unless you get him on his own. He's not the loudest voice, and certainly not the one most often heard during team talks, but when he makes a point it's usually a valid one.

There is nothing that I can coach him in with regard to the technicalities of the game. He's the complete player, a genius.

But he, like the others, needs direction. I try to give them alternatives to situations. We organise ourselves around the various types of situation that might develop in a game and try to sort out a plan to match it, to nullify it or take advantage of it. But, all the time, leaving room for improvisation. You have to with a team like we have.

Often, of course, I can see a situation building up and I know that this is just what we have practised time after time and what should come next. Then, because of this magnificent ability to improvise, somebody like Kidd will feint to do the obvious, say a pass inside to Bobby Charlton, jink back with that incredible body swerve of his and crack the ball in the net.

And I'm left with a curse dying on my lips and saying: "Keep your mouth shut, Mal."

Even the best players in the world need direction and organisation and if I have a strength it's the ability to promote that sort of scheme.

I hesitated to be forceful with Bobby Charlton.

Here was a man of 33, with his immense experience and with more than 100 England caps. He was working himself into the ground, running those legs weary trying to cover every part of the field. And he wasn't being beneficial to the team; he was negating his own strength and skill with total involvement in everybody else's job.

He was covering behind the full-backs, attacking and shooting up front and trying to get things moving in midfield and he was, frankly, doing far too much. In fact he was working so hard that he could well have finished himself for ever by the end of season 1970–71.

When I broached the subject with him and told him I'd be moving somebody else alongside him in the middle of the park he thought about it for a moment and then quickly agreed with my suggestion. Now, for a man of his vast experience to accept my suggestion without demur was a heartening experience, the mark of a man who has only United's interest uppermost in his mind.

It was all so simple really. Bobby was trying to do everything for Manchester United and it was not humanly possible for him to accept, and survive, so much responsibility.

Now Bobby plays more to the left of the field and is a bit more organised with somebody to help him out, somebody to share the load. It helped to stop him over-doing the hard work factor and gave him a new lease of life.

He's not only a danger in the middle—he's been given more freedom to go forward and have a shot at goal and that, in itself is a reward for the fans. He is still one of the most exciting players in the world, never mind England or even Europe.

If he has a fault it is his emotional involvement; he gets upset quickly, but that's only frustration if things are not slotting into place or going right. But that's that mark of the top professional. He knows what *should* be happening and if it's not then he becomes angry at himself as much as anybody else because he can't seem to do anything about it.

Probably the greatest revelation of all the stars I have listed and analysed has surely been Willie

George Best . . . bootless in battle.

Morgan, a Scottish international at outside right and destined, in my view, to get more caps as a midfield player.

Willie's contribution to United's success has been immeasurable—but it can be even greater still if only he'll do what I want him to do. And that's go forward more to knock in a few more goals. But I can't get him to believe in himself as a goal-scorer; he'd prefer to lay it on for somebody else and he sees himself as a creator of chances rather than as a converter of them.

If there are five essential qualities for a midfield man then Willie has four of them. They need to be destroyers of the opposition attack, good passers of the ball, they need to have endless stamina, be a good runner and have the ability to win the ball. Willie is not a destroyer. But he has everything else.

When he was a winger he was nothing more than that. He wasn't too bothered about getting involved and, indeed, was in and out of the side. And I asked him to look hard at himself and rather than moan about the reserve football ask himself just why he wasn't in the first team.

He was honest enough to come up with the right answers—but had a further suggestion to offer. He wanted, he said, to go into midfield and told us that he had been a cross country runner as a youth and had stamina for the job. And he became probably the first of the men to be zoned at United. He also turned into a regular with a skill that has made him an ace in his new job.

His midfield partner Alan Gowling was an ordinary player with enough intelligence to know his limitations and enough good sense to accept a change, again at his own suggestion, that benefited everybody.

Alan and Willie, helping Bobby in the thick of the action, are now among the best pair of middle men in the business. They were handed new responsibilities and accepted them gladly.

Alan, big and strong, replaced Brian Kidd for a little while as a front runner but he couldn't turn quite so well as Brian is close situations—and there are few men better than Kiddo on the turn. But when Brian faded a little and Alan was

Musgrove in action as a West Ham winger.

Alan Gowling . . . good sense enough to accept a change that suited all.

slotted into his place he got mad about it—and it did him good. It perked him up and put him right back on his toes.

We have the problem of age hanging like a black cloud over some of our best players and we are constantly reminded of it . . . but even though Denis and Bobby are over thirty they will still be in the top flight for at least another two years and, by then, the rich harvest of youngsters will have blossomed out of the reserves.

Look at Sammy McIlroy. He's got everything you'd ever want in a young player, speed, strength, stamina, a great shot, heading ability and a skill beyond his years in reading the game. He's a deadly finisher and could easily replace Denis Law, or take George Best's role. And he could also fill in naturally any gap left by Bobby Charlton. He is three players in prospect. And there are still more youngsters developing in his wake.

The blend will come again alright without too

much of a gap in it's development: the youngsters will gradually be slotted in beside the more experienced players and will learn as they go along and they'll soon get used to United's traditional trend for success.

The thing is that at Old Trafford we tend not to stereotype our players, we prefer to allow them to stretch themselves from their own reserves of skill and talent while organising them into a unit. United have always had a reputation for attracting the sort of player who has individual flair, men like Bobby Charlton, Denis Law, Brian Kidd and George Best, and this pattern will quite obviously continue.

But the boss and I, while still urging that development and that hunt for those types of players, will fashion them into more of an organised unit around their individuality.

This heartening progression can easily be seen in Sammy McIlroy and the way he emerged both as an individualist and a complete team player when he stepped out for his senior debut against Manchester City at Maine-Road in the autumn of 1971.

With boys like this—and he was only 17 then—how can our system fail? There are many others I could name who fill most of the positions in the teams and, given time and patience, they will emerge just like Sammy did.

I try to further the relationship between myself and the players with a warmth of *bonhomie*, friendship: I want to be mates with them, but I also want them to know and understand fully who is the boss. I want suggestions, but I don't want my views questioned. I want respect—because that's what I give them.

I'm on the side of the players—and I make sure they know it. When the boss, Mr O'Farrell, gives them a telling off I'm the man they tell their troubles to. And I'm always going to listen . . . and I'll always have a sympathetic ear. But they'll get my views in with it as well.

There really is very little personality trouble at United, the players are world class, experienced and understanding. They know they are playing for the best club in the world, that its traditions demand loyalty and its fans deserve the finest football they can give. They have gone through most of the ups and downs that a footballer may experience, enjoyable or otherwise, and have learned how to react without bleating publicly about their teammates.

David Sadler, the quiet man at the heart of the side, deep in defence, locked inside his own half, after sampling some of the glories of forward play, is a model man to have in one of your shirts.

If he had a fault it was that he lacked a bit of aggression—and that's what I'm trying to inject in him without turning him into a dirty player. Hard but fair, that's how we want David and he'll be in Munich with England for the World Cup.

He listened patiently and with great appreciation of my suggestions that his aggression could be stronger and he accepted the advice, and took action on it, without retreating to the defence that he was capped for England without changing his mode of play.

When you give men like this an explanation, when you treat them as thinking individuals, which is what most of them are these days, then they give you something back. And that's interest in what you are trying to do for them—and, most important, the club they represent.

There is a natural zeal in most professionals and a sharply developed sense of responsibility; the psychiatry of the job is to spark it if it has gone a little dormant. That, in my view, is one of the essential factors of my job.

You don't have to shout and bawl at them; subtlety, without losing the point at issue, is a nice weapon to have in your armoury. I've tried to include it in mine.

I think I have got the finest job in football anywhere in the world. Manchester United, despite what my old mate Malcolm Allison has said, are a fine team.

What they are not is a one man side. That I heard many times and I cannot imagine a view further from accuracy than that.

We have won games without George Best, without Brian Kidd and without Denis Law; we won them with an almost completely reserve defence. We won them with team work, skill and determination that sprang with life out of a side of deep character.

Manchester United are going to go from strength to strength and, I forecast, be a strong force in Europe again. That is my vow—and Frank O'Farrell's instruction. . . .

Teamwork is first in training at Old Trafford

Francis Lee . . . getting to grips.

ACTION MEN: CHRIS LAWLER (Liverpool) ALAN GILZEAN (Spurs)

ACTION MEN: RAY KENNEDY (Arsenal) DENIS PARKIN (Wolves)

ACTION MEN:

ALAN BALL (left above) in action in his first game after moving to Arsenal.

COLIN HARVEY (Everton) beats PAUL REANEY (Leeds United) in a tackling duel.

Bobby Moore (back) watches action from Alan Bloor (Stoke) and Bobby Ferguson (West Ham).

JUST WHAT THE 'DOC' ORDERED

By
Billy
Bremner

Bremner down . . . but happy he's got a goal.

SCOTLAND'S days in the wilderness of international soccer achievement are coming to a close and we are, I sincerely believe, about to see the dawning of a triumphant side.

I have known tremendous success with Leeds United but as Scotland's skipper I have tasted only sour defeats and sad results, a situation which, I think, will alter drastically before the World Cup in Munich in 1974.

Now my objective, and Scotland's, too, is to make Munich, and world football in general, sit up and take notice when the World Cup comes round again.

There is hope, there is skill and talent and,

> **BILLY BREMNER, the Leeds United skipper whose Scottish aspirations have taken an upswing with the appointment of Tommy Docherty as the national team chief, talks about his feelings for Scotland and recalls the players he has met internationally and the problems they have brought him.**

above all, a fierce determination among all footballing Scots to achieve something great in world soccer and that means taking the Jules

Rimet trophy to Scotland for the first time in its history.

We Scots, once a force in international football, have slipped further back into the reckonings than we could ever have believed possible . . . now, mainly because of one man's fervour, we are on the threshold of revitalisation.

The man, of course, is Tommy Docherty, the fireball boss of Chelsea, the controversial manager of Rotherham United, Aston Villa and Queen's Park Rangers, the assistant at Hull City and the man who came back from the backwaters of Spanish football to take over as Scotland's team chief.

Docherty is my sort of man; he's forthright, he's tough, he's a football expert with ideas and schemes galore and he's a Scot with his national team's interests uppermost in his mind. And he is fired with the ambition to be successful.

In terms of absolute success I suppose the World Cup must be our aim. Here, both Tommy and I have known the humiliation, the frustration of failure and the misery of missing out when triumph had so many glories to offer.

Tommy, who earned two caps in the final stages of the World Cup in 1954 when it was staged in Switzerland, plainly has painful memories of that episode when it was the last-but-one time Scotland qualified.

They were bad times for Scotland; beaten 1–0 by Austria in Zurich and then given a terrible thrashing, 7–0 by the Uruguayans.

The team was hampered by all sorts of problems, not the least of which was the resignation of Andy Beattie, the Scots team manager, after the defeat by Austria.

Tommy, halfback in both defeats, couldn't have ever had a greater disappointment than when, in the second game, Uruguay put seven past us.

Scotland finished bottom of pool three, behind Uruguay, Austria and Czechoslovakia, without scoring a win, a point or even a single goal. It was a terrible time for us. . .

Four years later, in Sweden, we were bottom again, behind France, Yugoslavia and Paraguay in pool two. This time we scraped one point for a draw against Yugoslavia and scored one goal— but that was the last time we appeared in the final stages.

England, scene of the World Cup in 1966, came and went without us and so did Mexico four years later. Now Germany gives us another chance to make it good and to put Scotland's name back where it belongs, among the best of the world's national sides.

Twenty years after Scotland's most disastrous campaign in Switzerland and the Doc's one and only World Cup as a qualifier the wheel of fortune has turned a full circle—and he's back

Hoeness, of Bayern, a World Cup star?

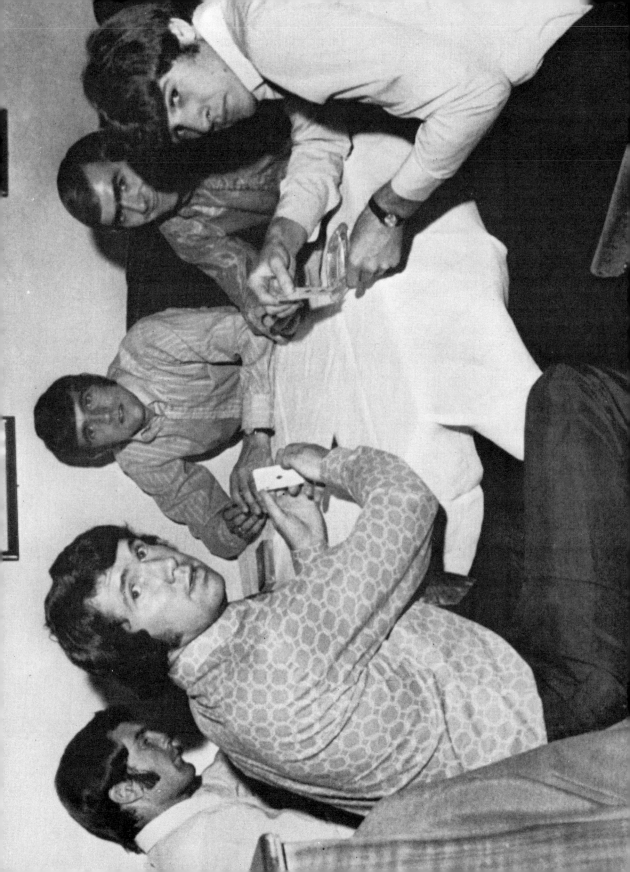

again, this time as the boss, the planner, the one man who could plot our progress all the way into the finals.

There cannot be a genuine Scot, anywhere in the world, who is not looking forward with a feeling of excitement to the oncoming international battles. The promise of great things to come, sparked by Tommy Docherty, gives me at least a great thrill of anticipation.

We have been too long on our knees as a football nation; we have known too much disappointment, too much failure and we are about to hit back under the Doc's inspiration.

I cannot praise him too highly; he did for Scotland, in 1971, what no other manager has managed to do for years, he got us believing in ourselves. He convinced every player in the squad that it is possible for Scotland to do what England did in 1966, win the World Cup.

He could do for us what Sir Alf Ramsey did for England: I hope so. This is probably my last chance for the greatest glory of all. I'm 29 now and, plainly, I can't expect to walk into the reckonings for the World Cup '78.

We reached the very bottom end of our confidence when our old foes, England, beat us 3–1 at Wembley in 1971; that May day defeat, in front of 100,000 spectators when Martin Chivers scored twice and Martin Peters notched the other one, was terrible for us. We never like being beaten by England—but this was too much.

Every player then in the Scotland squad was worried about our dismal record; the same players now, under Doc, really believe they can be considered among the elite of international teams.

The transformation, almost from the first minute we saw him as our boss, was immediate. I doubted that any man could make such an overnight success, but he did. . .

He's a great talker, a fierce emphasiser of his points and somehow got us thinking that every other team in the game would think they were privileged to even share the same area of turf as we did. And when we walked out to play Portugal we were twice the size we had been for years, confidence oozed from everyone of us.

Then, I suppose, because of the way we played, because of the promise I could see in the lads, I began to realise that the World Cup was not out of our reach. I knew that my great ambition to lead Scotland to World Cup victory was not as remote as we had begun to believe it was.

Of course, I have had terrific satisfaction and splendid success with Leeds United, and that, for many players, would be enough. But not for me. I am a Scot and national pride bursts from me. . .

It means a lot to me to play for Scotland, to pull that dark blue jersey over my head. And, I know, all the other lads feel the same way.

When the Munich battles come round I feel that my country will have built up a superb squad of around 30 players who will carry our crest with a pride that has been long gone, with an effectiveness that will make the other countries sit up and take notice.

But first, naturally, the "auld enemy" England, have to be sorted out. Bobby Charlton is as fervent for England as I am for Scotland and he knows exactly how I feel about victory in this game.

You'll probably get long odds on Scotland for Munich '74—so I think they'll be worth a bet. Get on to us before the bookies do!

These 'L' men no learners

All 'L' men but not one a learner. These five England players pictured at a quiet game of cards in Basle before the Switzerland match in 1971 are all from Leeds or Liverpool. Left to right: Paul Madeley, Chris Lawler, Norman Hunter, Terry Cooper, and Emlyn Hughes.

Two more Munich Men to Fear

Gerhard Muller of Bayern flashes in to score in the style that makes him high in the list of German probables for the next World Cup.

Wolfgang Overath . . . and cups for the lads.

When it's all those thousands it needs thinking about

Harry Catterick, Everton manager . . . deep in thought.

Alan Ball of Everton . . . off to a new world with Arsenal for a fee of £225,000.

The TOUGH line —How tough?

I WILL be interested to see how many defenders appear on the lists of players not to be retained by their clubs when the next few successive seasons come to a close.

There will be quite a few I would imagine. For the new clamp-down and harsher punishment for soccer's offenders is liable to draw all the teeth of men who specialise in defence.

I feel sorry for defenders. I think the new rule has been too harshly interpreted, the defenders are suffering and, I believe, the game is, too.

I agree that some sort of action was necessary but I think it could have been done more objectively with referees given a bigger chance for judgement on the field, according to each separate game, rather than applying rigid laws and punishments to every situation.

Some tackles from the back can be really wounding and unfair while others can be carried out neatly and fairly with the ball being won cleanly by a defender.

I have always been against changes that alter the tradition of the game; this has been one of them.

It is, after all a man's game and it needs physical contact. Soon we'll have teams without defenders, with only attackers who don't tackle and possession never won or earned only given by the other side's errors.

What a dreadful bore that would turn out to be. There are a few players who can only be defenders who are tough and with a penchant for hard tackling. They, for my money, are part of the

BOBBY CHARLTON

gives his view of the clamp down by referees that gave 1971 its biggest soccer controversy

game. An essential part. They can be controlled by referees—but not neutralised altogether.

They are in danger of becoming redundant. A tragic thought for they have been part of the British soccer scene since the game began.

Look at men like Bolton's defenders Roy Hartle and Tommy Banks—they were as hard as nails. You knew you'd been in a game with them. They didn't do football any harm at all—and they did it many favours by sparking players they tackled into stepping lively and teaching them a greater awareness.

When I played as an orthodox left winger I

48

Where's the ball? Stoke City v. Ipswich.

GETS FIERCE

The goalie's missed it . . . Hull City v. Brentford.

Over the top . . . in a Leeds game.

used to hope and pray that the fullback would come after me and come after me hard. I wanted him to commit himself and then I could wait for him, slip the ball past him and get away with one man usually on the floor and out of the game behind me.

The fullbacks I had trouble with were not these hard cases but the men who positioned themselves and tried to run me out of the game.

There was also the greater opportunity to earn free kicks to get possession; this is another aspect of the game which is likely to fade.

Every winger knew, and appreciated, that every fullback was going to make sure in the first few minutes that you knew you were in for a hard time—and I don't think the game suffered one iota for this sort of play.

There are players like Brian O'Neill at Southampton, who is known as one of the game's toughest tacklers. He is lucky. He has enough skill to change his style and cut out the tougher stuff. But there are other players who simply cannot alter—and they'll be robbed of employment.

Nowadays, for instance, you know as a professional that you are going to have possession from every throw-in. The defender just dare not challenge.

The thrower merely aims the ball at a teammate, who doesn't even have to run into space, and you know that the tackle from the opposing defender is not going to come. One from behind is illegal.

What sort of game is it where a challenge from that type of situation is not allowed? Not the sort I'd like to be watching in ten years time when my playing days are over.

I'll be like the rest of the fans then. I'll want to put on my red and white scarf, go down to Old Trafford and watch some action, some men's stuff. Not two teams rushing about, not tackling each other and just waiting for the other side to make a mistake and send a pass wrong so they can get the ball.

That's not the sort of football I want to see and I am sure the fans don't either.

I think the change has been too rigidly enforced and once it has become established I can't see the league changing it back again.

I'm all for goals, and the new regulations have done something about that: but I'm old fashioned, too. I like my football the way I have grown up with it. I don't like too many changes—and this is one too many the way it is being applied.

If I were a defender I'd be worried about my future right now.

The responsibility must be handed back to the man on the spot, the referee. He must be made to be stronger with decisions on this issue left entirely up to him, not left to enforce inflexible rules that leave no room for initiative.

You have, of course, to defend the good and clever players and make sure they are adequately protected from kickers—but don't pull out all the defenders' teeth. Give them room for a little bite. This is not a game for timid men.

The most difficult part of the game of football is to get the ball—it's also one of the most exciting and manly parts of the game to try and win it. Without tackling, or with tackling opportunities lessened, the chance to get the ball for your own side becomes an increasingly difficult task.

The only way, really, to stamp out dirty play, not hard, fair play but clean play, is to get players to behave themselves. And I don't subscribe to the view that this is impossible.

I would urge the planners to modify their ideas, good as they are fundamentally, but do it soon before the game deteriorates into one which loses all its spectacle and all its great competitive spirit and challenge.

THERE'S
A TIME
FOR
SWINGIN'

CLOWNING

. . . with Jimmy Greaves on an England tour.

FLYING

. . . with Nobby Stiles and Shay Brennan on a club tour.

TALKING

and, of course, just
the odd bit of

PLAYING

On Australian tour...

In match action.

ONE IN THE EYE

. . . and Stoke City's Jimmy Greenhoff is on the receiving end of this one.

The way a boss teaches his stars

The boss who makes sure things are one right. Pictured on the left is Manchester City team boss Malcolm Allison in a training session with first team keeper Joe Corrigan here pictured doing in practice what he achieves so spectacularly when the tough competition is on.

Now a step or two down memory lane

Dennis Viollet scores against Newcastle United in a 1956 League game at Old Trafford.

An England team (above) and a Manchester United team (below). The names, page 126.

Tommy Taylor.

Snow clearing with Dennis Viollet, Bill Foulkes, and Freddie Goodwin.

A venture into Rugby League . . . listening to Alex Murphy, international star.

Nelson[?] for a world beat[?]: Ferenc Puskas (centre) at a London dinner.

Coming home to win

BY GEORGE EASTHAM

'The greatest moment of my career was when I knocked in the League Cup final winner for Stoke at Wembley'

MY long span of soccer experience has covered a great many changes and has taken me to far-off places—but when I returned home from one of my farthest trips away from home two great things happened: There was a crack down on tough play; I won a League Cup winner's medal at Wembley.

I had been asked to take up a player-manager's position with a team in Capetown, South Africa, and for nine months I was away from the hurly-burly of British football and playing in the rather less strenuous atmosphere of the football 6,000 miles from home.

But even while I was away my boss at Stoke City, Tony Waddington, was frequently on the telephone to me, his voice crackling on the radio link, telling me all about the game back home and, of course, that revolution.

It was, you will have guessed by now, the new law that meant the cracking down on tough play . . . the referee's charter that was taking a lot of the sting out of the British game.

The boss, who had so understandingly released me to Capetown for their season, kept asking me: "When will you be back here?"

And he added: "You just won't believe it when you get back. The way things have changed it's incredible. The ref's are really cracking down on the rough stuff."

I flew home on a Monday night in October, 1971, and on the following Wednesday I was on the substitute's bench for a league cup game against Manchester United at Old Trafford. And I couldn't believe my eyes. . .

Tony Waddington had told me all about the change, as I have said, but I could not believe just how severely things had changed until I sat, getting more and more surprised, watching from the Old Trafford sidelines.

I wondered what the hell had happened to the game as I had known it for fourteen years. Two players were booked for tackles that would hardly have warranted a rebuke the season before.

And here I must share Bobby's views, which he has expressed somewhere else in this book, that sometimes change is not a good thing. Like him I suppose I am a traditionalist.

I have grown up in the game as it was and I felt something had been taken from it.

People have told me: "It must be great for you now, George. You'll be able to stay in the game much longer now that those sort of tackles have been negated by the ref's."

Well, it doesn't make any difference whatever to me. I am still playing in the way I have always done, and that means whether I've been getting whacked or not.

George and Bobby forget their friendship.

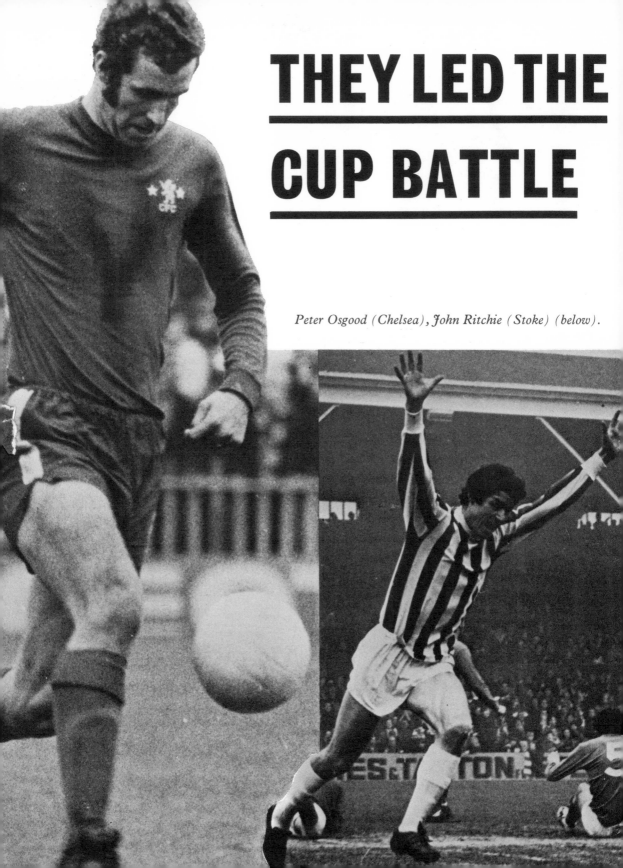

THEY LED THE
CUP BATTLE

Peter Osgood (Chelsea), John Ritchie (Stoke) (below).

I don't stop to think now that I can do something more because I'm not going to be tackled from behind: what I do, and what I have always done, is instinctive, on the spur of the moment and without any thought or regard for the tackle that might come.

In that respect the new law, despite what advantages people *imagine* it gives me, has done nothing to help me. My game is just the same.

I agree that ball players need protection and that the dirty stuff should be cut out—but I also believe that it did no harm to be whacked hard, as long as it was fair and not done in a nasty, sneaky fashion.

I have had my share of bangings over the years and it has never really bothered me. I took it as part of the game. And, even if the game had still been hard I would still have wanted to play as long as I could.

I hold the opinion that sometimes when a player gets tumbled hard it sets him alight, it sparks him, it causes something inside him to come alive and he's often a better man for it.

I can take all of this and get on with the game. I've certainly not been put out of the game for any long periods because of this sort of tackle.

Spectators seem to have me marked as a frail man, in the way that if there is a cold wind I go back into the house to put my overcoat on. Well, the wind doesn't blow right through me. I might be slight—but frail, no. I train as hard as any other professional in the game, and enjoy it too.

Though, I must say, I loved the weather in South Africa when I was with Hellenic Capetown. The game is such there that I never needed to knock myself out to keep up the pace. And that was really a fast game.

There was very little tackling, not so much physical contact as at home and, consequently, the game was a lot faster though not strenuous.

And, for the first time in my life, I got my hands on some trophies. We won the league and a couple of other cups, too. It was the first time they had tasted such triumph and I enjoyed steering them towards it all. I'd never won anything in my life until I played out there.

And then, to top it all, I was voted Footballer of the Year! It could only happen in South Africa. . .

The South Africa soccer scene is one which I feel will probably attract even more players from Britain once the word gets round.

It's not fully professional, and that's the only aspect of it which fails to appeal to me because I am an addict of the professional game, but it pays awfully good money.

Most of the players, and the club officials, for that matter, are part-timers. But the players are earning money that would rival some of the wages offered by our own first division clubs.

It's possible for the South African clubman to pick up £100-a-week easy money. And when I think how I used to have to flog myself into the ground for twenty quid a week!

They are playing in front of gates of 20,000 and more—and once we pulled in 40,000 fans. The South Africans really do love their football.

With no television—it hasn't reached there yet—live soccer is a terrific attraction. And the fever in Capetown, where they have two teams, rivals anything felt on Merseyside or in Manchester.

The teams travel far and wide across the country—and that was something which really appealed to me. I love travel and I got plenty of it over there.

Capetown is the furthest end of the country and we had to journey to Durban, a thousand miles away; East London which was 750 miles off and Port Elizabeth, 500 miles from home.

Sometimes we used to cover a 2,000 miles round trip to Durban and home again by jet in a day! How about that?

We could get the team out of bed at home in Capetown at about six o'clock in the morning and fly them off to Durban. Then we could put them back to bed by about 9 am for a rest before the game. . .

As soon as we were safely on the ground we would get the team fixed up for a meal and rest at a hotel—the flight would take only two hours or so which was quicker, and less tiring, too, than travelling say from Manchester to London by train.

Everything about South Africa appealed to me. My wife and I had a superb penthouse flat overlooking the city with glorious views. We had a maid and a car and all the comforts anybody could wish for—and everything was so much cheaper than in England.

We were close to the beach and unless you have seen those South African beaches it would be hard to understand and appreciate just how much of a reward that is.

We used to train the team for only an hour a night; as most of them were fixed up in full-time day jobs we didn't want to flatten them with arduous training schedules when they had finished their usual employment.

The football is not of a tremendous standard, but it's good enough to excite the crowds. But it's the sort of game that means a good, fit British player could go on playing for a few years after he would have retired at home.

It all seemed a far cry from those black old days ten years or so ago when I made my stand against the Football League for higher wages—when the maximum was eventually lifted after I'd very nearly put myself out of the game for good.

I was happy to do it—but the agony of being out of football for so long, while the court wrangles and arguments with the league went on, just about killed me. I was the gloomiest man in Britain in the early sixties. The fact that I won my point, that I saw my principles and my own personal anguish finally rewarded, was compensation enough for me.

I had to get another job outside the game and times were really hard because my wife and I had just had our first child. And not being allowed to play the game I loved almost as much as life upset me even more.

Since then, of course, players' wages have soared to almost unbelievable heights—and quite rightly so. We are entertainers who keep thousands of people occupied and interested every weekend.

Aside from that League Cup winners' goal at Wembley my personal achievements could, I suppose, be numbered nineteen. They are the number of international caps I won with England. I don't have a trophy cupboard, there's nothing to put in it except those awards from South Africa.

But I can say I played in a Wembley final which is every player's ambition. But what's even more important I played there for England—against fabulous Brazil in a 1–1 draw in 1963.

Then I followed it up by being selected against Czechoslovakia, East Germany in the same year—

Down goes Terry Conroy, Stoke City and Eire international wing star.

and, in 1964, I played against Wales, Northern Ireland, Scotland, the Rest of the World, Uruguay, Portugal, Eire, America, when we won 10–0 in New York, Brazil, in Rio de Janeiro, when we lost 5–1 and Argentina, another great team who beat us 1–0, again in Rio.

My international career carried on through 1965, though my appearances dropped to three with matches against West Germany, at Nuremberg when we beat them 1–0; Hungary at Wembley and against Sweden in Gothenberg, another win, this time 2–1.

It all ended in 1966 with my final three internationals against Spain in Madrid, Poland at Liverpool and, alas, my departure from the scene against Denmark in Copenhagen.

But, at least, I went out with some little glory. I scored. The second goal I had notched for England—the other being against Eire in Dublin two years before.

My caps seemed to come just when I had given up all hope of ever being selected for my country. I had been playing on what I considered to be a peak of form when Walter Winterbottom was in charge of England—but he favoured Johnny Haynes, my rival for the international place, and I simply could not get in.

I even went in the squad to Chile for the World Cup in 1962—but Haynes held his place. England were whacked 3–1 in the Quarter Finals at Vina del Mar, when Garrincha scored two glorious goals. They went on to win the Cup when they beat Czechoslovakia by the same score in Santiago.

It seemed to me that I was to be the permanent skip carrier along with Harold Shepherdson, the England trainer. I had played for my country at the Under-23 level—but I couldn't make the senior side under Mr Winterbottom.

I was playing as well as anybody, but Johnny Haynes had the job and that was that. I had resigned myself to that fact.

But along came Alf Ramsey, as the new England boss, and he put me into the team for that memorable match against those super players from Brazil at Wembley. After that one

England star striker Geoff Hurst shows his getaway style to Manchester City's Tommy Booth.

game seemed to follow another and my international ambitions all came to fruition.

That is, of course, until I handed over my shirt to Roger Hunt, the Liverpool striker, who played in the number ten jersey for a great number of games afterwards.

It was during this period that I became really friendly with the two men who among all footballers are my two firmest pals, Bobby Charlton and my teammate at Stoke, Gordon Banks.

Bobby played outside left to me for a while—and I could see what a great player he was. And

what a shot, too! I watched him score some fabulous goals and have admired him for his skill and sportsmanship ever since.

And what a magnificent goalkeeper Gordon Banks is. I know full well that he has received just about every compliment there is, but I feel I must add my own bit in singing his praises.

Having played in the same team as him at Stoke I have had plenty of time to assess him as a goalkeeper, both in training and in the matches proper.

I must report that almost every week I have watched him he has done something, pulled out some save or uncannily read a situation, and I have been left wondering how on earth he does it.

We at Stoke have always felt that when he was in the side we were certainly good for at least a draw—because we felt that even if we forwards didn't manage to knock in any goals at least he would not be letting in any goals at the back.

That is the sort of confidence he instills in everybody whether it is at club level or on the international front.

The save of his that kept us in the Football League Cup at West Ham, early in 1972, was out of this world and every bit as good as the sensational one he pulled off against Pele in Mexico in the World Cup.

At West Ham, facing up to a Geoff Hurst penalty—and Geoff can really bang them hard—Gordon flung himself to his right and somehow, I'll never know how, he knocked the ball over the top. Of course, the way Geoff hits them it only takes a slight touch of the ball to send it off course . . . but you've got to get the touch!

Gordon did okay—and Geoff, his England teammate, was left with a gloomy hangdog expression on his face. Gordon gambled but was quick to move, too. He guessed right and his action was sharp enough to make it pay off.

How can you ever believe you will lose with a goalkeeper like that playing behind you? He must be worth two goals start in any match.

We kid him on a lot, about his luck, about his knack of managing to be in the right place and suggesting that he's usually trying to get out of the way rather than in the path of a penalty from a man like Hurst. But he takes it all in good part.

The most punishing aspect of Gordon's ability is the fact that we expect him to make this sort of save all the time. He has set himself such a high standard that we never expect him to fall below it—and he rarely does. When he is beaten you can bet your life that there is not a goalkeeper in the world who would have stopped it.

Of course he has his off days, and this is only to be expected, but they are so few and far between that his brilliance seems to glow continually.

Imagine having two friends like these: Bobby,

Mike Pejic.

one of the world's most gifted players, and Gordon, probably the finest goalkeeper there ever was. And both of them oddball characters with a neat line in humour and good sense enough not to allow all the adulation go to their heads.

It's small wonder that even though I'm England's oldest forward—incidentally marginally ahead of Bobby!—that I don't want to quit the game. Ever. . .

Bayern Munich ace Hoeness and Liverpool's Tommy Smith.

MERSEYSIDE MEN:

Chris Lawler, Britain's top scoring full back, shows how it's done against West Ham United.

Joe Royle, Everton, beats Dennis Clarke, Huddersfield Town defender, in this Goodison clash.

MERSEYSIDE MEN:

Roger Kenyon and Henry Newton (No. 3). Alan Gilzean grounded.

Sir Alf Ramsey.

SIR ALF CAN GET THE CAPS TO FIT

BOBBY CHARLTON looks at the two players who, in his opinion, have improved by leaps and bounds and have put themselves on the fringe of England international recognition.

TWO players who in my opinion really shot into the reckonings as class men in the 1971–72 season were, coincidentally, both in the second half of their twenties.

And this time of life, so far as footballers go, is probably the peak time of a career. The time when you are playing better than you have ever done before.

It happened to me: I reckon that when I was turned 25 I really began to play the game with better understanding and with greater efficiency than I had ever shown before.

This, I believe, is what has happened to the two players who have taken my vote as the most improved players around.

They are David Wagstaffe, transferred to Wolves from Manchester City, and Howard Kendall, another transferred player, from Preston North End to Everton.

Wagstaffe, an out-and-out winger with a devastating shot and real close control, would walk into any England team . . . if wingers were the fashion.

Howard Kendall and Roy McFarland.

Derek Dougan (Wolves) and Terry Cooper (Leeds United).

He is the finest left winger in Britain—and, when for a long time he was only moderate, an average sort of player, he has suddenly bloomed as one of the game's great players.

Malcolm Allison, Manchester City's team manager, must rue the day that one of his predecessors sold Wagstaffe. For Malcolm's problems with Manchester City seemed to have revolved around the left side of the field and a player like Wagstaffe would plainly leave no room for worry about that department.

Whenever we have played Wolves Wagstaffe has given us no end of trouble and other players I have spoken to have said he did the same with their teams.

His left foot is so deadly and his long crosses so accurate that he spells danger as soon as he gets anywhere near the ball: men like Hugh Curran and Derek Dougan have benefited more with him than they probably would have done with anybody else.

Once he had turned 25—and I think he's now into that second phase of his twenties—then Wagstaffe seemed to find more time to do everything. He became unhurried and apparently less troubled by defenders. He made sure he took more time to do what he wanted—at his pace.

The long experience he has had, allied to his natural skills, have turned him into a formidable footballer. The fact that his right foot seems to be a "swinger" doesn't bother him—and I don't believe it should.

I am not a firm advocate of the feeling that footballers should be two-footed. Obviously it is better if they are—but if you have one great foot like Wagstaffe's you don't have to worry.

For my money he was the sensation of the 1971–72 season. Every time I saw him, sometimes on television, he just seemed to get better.

It was the same with Howard Kendall. What a player he is! He seems to have been around for years and, of course, he has been playing for a long time. But he, too, has turned that 25 mark and, with the added task of Everton's captaincy, he has stepped into the mould of greatness.

He's been great for Dougan . . .

Kendall had always been a good defender, a willing worker and a man to give 101 percent effort all the time. Then, when Alan Ball was transferred to Arsenal, Harry Catterick gave Howard Ball's skippership.

'That seemed to be the trick that added even more to his maturity; the responsibility was no weight on his shoulders. On the contrary he carried it lightly and fed on it to add to his stature as a player.

Kendall is not only a superb defender but when he is going forward to the front edge of the penalty area he can be among the most dangerous goalscorers around. I have seen him knock in some great goals from way out—and now he looks as if he could be doing more of that, accepting even more responsibility than he's been asked to undertake.

It is a great pity that there are so many halfbacks around to keep Kendall away from the frontline of Sir Alf Ramsey's England selection.

Both Howard and David have reached a consistency, a very high standard, that suggests they will be around for a long time to come. And I can think of two team managers who will be extremely happy men to have such a basis of skill to weave into their sides.

The 25-years-old-and-on age group seems more and more to produce players who have come of age in the business of football. At that stage of the game you seem to think less and less about what you are doing and allow movements and actions to become more natural and more spontaneous.

It serves to cover the old saying: you cannot beat experience!

Mick Jones.

THEY'RE TOPS IN WORLD SOCCER

BILLY BREMNER picks his world's best . . . and Britain's best.

IT would be impossible to compile any sort of dossier on the world's top five forwards without putting the magical Pele down as defenders' enemy number one.

I believe that some of my views on the players I have chosen will not fit in with those held by any other players or spectators—and I am sure that my choice even will not match up to that of the great majority.

The fact is that these are all players I have matched wits with, fellows with reputations that have been justified by their own ability and who have made the football world sit up and take notice. And who have made defenders like me wish they could all be on my side.

I have played against Pele only once—and I would dearly love to be matched against him at least once more. Now, alas, because of his retirement as an international I am never going to realise that great ambition.

If he had stayed on as a player for Brazil, who knows I might have been marking him in a Brazil-Scotland World Cup Final in Munich. I have talked about my World Cup hopes for Scotland elsewhere in Bobby's book so I won't dwell on that point.

My confrontation with Pele, and it was certainly a tough one, happened just before the World Cup in 1966 and the great strolling Brazilians brought their sinewy skills to Hampden Park for a warm-up game with Scotland. We Scots didn't view it as a friendly and we wanted to win. That's what the game is all about—winning.

I had good cause to remember Pele before the game was finished. He gave me a black eye!

So he, quite clearly, was not treating the Hampden match as any sort of friendly encounter.

It happened in a goalmouth tussle. He and I and Bobby Clark, the goalkeeper, went up for a ball and Pele seemed to be head and shoulders above the pair of us and still going up as we struggled to squeeze him out.

But while we were up there he gave me the elbow across my face and I finished up with a painful shiner. He had become needled as the game went on.

It was the only time we had ever played the Brazilians and I suppose we wanted to do well whether they were involved in the World Cup or not. And that June night in Glasgow seemed to be a good opportunity to show that we could do something as well.

Pele's reputation came before him: I had seen him on television and on film shots but I'd never seen him in the flesh before and, when I stood alongside him for the first time, I was amazed to see that he was not such a big fellow as I had imagined. Well, he wasn't so tall as he looks, probably around 5ft. 8ins—but what a build!

He had shoulders like a heavyweight boxer, wide and muscular and a great big deep chest. And his legs were as sturdy as oak. He was plainly going to be a hard man to shift off the ball. And I wasn't the first defender to discover that.

I wasn't in awe of him, I didn't think too much about his terrific reputation as the world's finest footballer because when you do that you are half-way to losing out. I simply got on with the game in the way I know best, tackling hard, quick and with sureness and not allowing the man to settle on the ball.

It seemed to upset him. And he became extremely niggled and, after a while, wouldn't take me on. He stayed clear. I suppose, quite rightly, he didn't want to risk any injuries with the World Cup so near.

But I followed him everywhere. And whenever the ball came near him I was on to it like a flash, harrying him, pressuring him into mistakes. I had worked it out that you cannot allow a man like him to settle or get too much of the ball because he will murder you.

I suppose this is why he became so upset—a point which I couldn't really appreciate because when you are a man with a reputation like his you

87

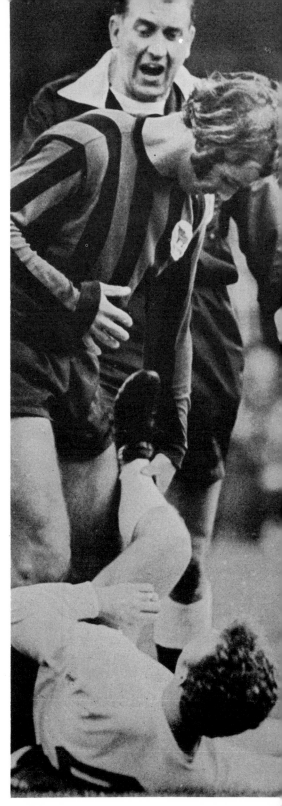

Bremner (below) and Jimmy Nicholson (Huddersfield).

must expect this sort of treatment and accept it as part of the game.

I do not believe he tried too hard but even though the tempo of the Brazil game was to be one where they exposed themselves to as little risk as possible he was still competitive, he still wanted to win. And was keen enough on that end to give me the elbow.

Many spectators feel sorry for him, he used to get hit so hard and so often, but they seem to forget that he was quite adept and certainly quite capable of giving back as good as he got. He was no softie and could look after himself as well as any so-called hard defender.

The aspect of his play which impressed me most was his really remarkable speed and acceleration. He looked fast when I saw him on film and when you are down there on the same park as him, trying to keep watch on him, his speed is almost unbelievable.

In a split second it seems he is backing onto the defender, unbalancing him, putting him off, but all the time backing on. Then in a flash he's gone . . . thirty yards away . . . powering along on those great legs and fast becoming a vanishing figure as you try to match his acceleration.

He can receive a ball with his back to you, you move in trying to get it and suddenly he snaps off and veers round, just as quickly, lays off a one-two or has a shot of incredible power.

His ability in the air, too, is something to be seen at close quarters to be really believed. He looks good from the terraces, but from close range he's fantastic. I suppose Gordon Banks would testify to that. It took the save of a lifetime from him in Mexico to keep Pele from scoring with a header of perfect quality.

When I went up with him and was on my way

Allan Clarke.

down again it seemed to me that he was still soaring upwards, he seemed to hang in the air, his timing is faultless.

He is among the most difficult of players to keep tabs on. He seems, like most of the world's top players, to have a radius of vision that is not granted to us mere mortals. In this respect he's like Bobby Charlton and George Best. These players appear to see things in wider range than other players. It's an indefinable quality peculiar to men of their calibre.

They can somehow see further to the sides and can, because of this gift, skip tackles just when you think you have got them, and can sling passes round apparently without looking where they are aiming.

We finished the game 1–1. Pele did not score and I suppose in that respect my job was done with some measure of success. But I would dearly love to meet him again in a game that meant something, a game like a World Cup fixture where we could really get to grips with one another.

I applied the same rules I had used against Pele when I met up with that other great man of football, Eusebio of Portugal. He, like Pele, is a legend, a super player who deserves special treatment when you meet up with him. Leave him for a second and you are in trouble.

We played Portugal in the Nations Cup and it was my job to look after Eusebio's interests in the game. At the time I felt that his enthusiasm for the game as a whole was on the wane. And, it seemed, that once I'd hit him hard a couple of times and showed I intended to be in command, he lost all his go and determination.

Eusebio, a world apart from Pele, plays much deeper without the Brazilian's hunger for involvement around the goalmouth. He's got a great shot and can swerve it which ever way he chooses, but he prefers to play deeper without knocking himself out with effort. At least that's the way it was when we met in Lisbon.

I don't think he moved at more than a stroll at any point of the game and was never breathing heavy. Four years ago, or around the World Cup

time, he was a great competitor, just a fierce as Pele.

But in 1971 all that had gone. It was as if he felt he had made all the money he wanted and wasn't too bothered about pulling out all the stops in any sort of concentrated effort.

There were times when he did something with the ball, again because of this radius of vision I have been writing about, when he looked like a player of extraordinary development. Then, just as quickly, it seemed to die. And he lapsed, keeping out of my way and finally caused us very little trouble at all.

I expected him to fight for everything and was keyed up to that sort of battle, just as it had been between him and Nobby Stiles when they met and clashed as old foes. Eusebio was another man with a reputation for being full-blooded and nobody's pushover, a player who could adequately look after himself.

He, like Pele, is a player I'd like to meet under more competitive circumstances. Maybe the story would be different, one of excitement rather than disappointment.

Whereas Pele was prepared to take all the abuse and all the knocks up front Eusebio seemed more anxious to retreat deeper and deeper into midfield, making the occasional break instead of being nippy around the penalty area.

Two great players for sure—but equalled in many ways by the men who are still very much in the game, the players on the home front.

Smiling Bobby.

George Best demonstrates his incredible control.

Now that Pele has quit George Best, Manchester United's wayward genius, is in my view the world number one footballer. It's almost a cliche to say it but there is no other way to describe him.

That title is the top accolade and it is not lightly given by other professionals. George is number one. There is no doubt about that and the emphasis is not exagerrated.

To play against George is an experience that you are unlikely to forget. You can smother him with tackles, you can play him close, hit him hard,

stop him getting the ball, you can nudge him, run him out and generally make it uncomfortable for him. Then you can settle back, think you have done a grand job and leave him for a second—and you are a goal down.

He is a man you cannot ever afford to ignore; he's a match winner from the quarter chance offered maybe only once in a game which you think you have won.

There is no part of the game that he has not mastered; aside from his groundskills he is one of the best headers of a ball in the business. When

Mike Pejic versus George Best.

you face up to him, guarding your goal, and he is coming at you there is absolutely no way at all of knowing which way he is going to go.

You can be certain in your mind when you are watching him carefully that you have twigged his plans, you can convince yourself that he has committed himself and make a lunge—and all you are left with is a muddy seat to your shorts and he's gone.

He seems to lean so far over that he will fall to the ground, it seems he will never get up again and then, you believe, is the time to move in. But up he comes, almost from the floor, leaning the other way and he's round you. I don't know how he does it.

It's the same with the wee man, my old friend Jimmy Johnstone, the Celtic winger, who is another genius.

It takes a player of exceptional skills to give my Leeds United colleague Terry Cooper any trouble. For my money Terry is the best left back in the business, he's fast, can tackle and is able to read situations as quick as any of the full-backs in the game's history.

But the wee man, Jimmy Johnstone, gave him, and the rest of us defenders for that matter, a real roasting at Hampden Park when Leeds United played Celtic in the European Cup Semi-Final in the 1969–70 season.

Jimmy was on peak form that night and poor Terry couldn't get anywhere near him: he was the jinking genius, murderously skilful, determined to do well and convinced that he could take on the whole Leeds United side on his own if necessary. And, on top of all this, I don't think he put a single ball wrong with his final pass.

He simply slaughtered us. We had no answer to him. And I don't think any fullback in the business would have had either.

I rate Cooper as good as Ray Wilson was and as good as that other great fullback Faccheti, the Italian, but even with a defender as masterly as he there was no answer to Johnstone. In that mood I have seen him go past eight and nine men and still looking for somebody to beat.

But, like all geniuses, and just like George Best, a man I have always admired and have always enjoyed playing against, wee Jimmy has his ups and downs. If they're on top of their game there is no holding them, if they feel out of it on the day then they can sink to terribly low levels. But just the same you have to watch them every second, one lapse on the defender's part and all is lost.

Both Best and Johnstone have incredible ball control, something you are born with, not something you can learn to the level they have mastered. Best I suppose, is the more complete of the pair.

All of the men I have mentioned are dynamic players who can generate excitement not only among fans but among professional footballers, too. They are all hot-headed, the penalty, I suppose of their fame and ability and the close marking it quite naturally brings.

I know it is difficult for them but they just have to accept that if the world ratings are such that they figure in the top half dozen players in the world then they must suffer the fact that every other player in the business wants to make sure they don't make him look foolish.

I have considered all the various aspects of their individual play and believe that they are truly geniuses at their own game—but the man, the really great striker of them all for my money, is the player I am leaving to the last.

He is my teammate Allan Clarke, the slim wraith of a man, who is the most gifted striker I have ever seen. Clarke is superb, a tremendous competitor, fearless despite his lack of weight, quick and with a stealth of movement that defies harnessing tactics.

His game may not be quite so complete as the others—but as a striker, pure and simple he is the best there is. He loves to see the ball thudding into the back of the net—and even in practice when he knocks one home you'd think it was the Cup Final winner he'd just struck.

He has only to get sight of the net, however frantic the action in the penalty area, and you can almost put your wages on the fact that the ball is going to end up there. He is uncanny and so

Goalscoring link (left to right); Ferenc Puskas, Hungarian goalscoring star, shakes hands with Francis Lee, watched by former Minister of Sport Dennis Howells.

elegant. He even falls with an elegance that gives him the appearance of a man who is going down still in complete control of his body.

I would dread having to mark Allan—he has that ghosting quality that John White, the late great Scottish International, possessed. He can get himself into scoring positions without the opposition noticing.

I remember walking out side by side with the England team when Scotland played them at Wembley—and I noticed with relief that Allan was not among the men selected to play. He was sitting it out on the subs' bench and I still reckon that it was a great let-off for us. We lost 3–1 in any case. I shudder to think what the score might have been had he played.

HOW MUCH FOR THIS ELEVEN?

(Left to right): Martin Chivers, Peter Storey, Ray Kennedy, Martin Peters, Francis Lee, Gordon Banks, Ron Davies, Frank McLintock, Billy Bremner, Bobby Moore, Chris Lawler.

GETTING MOSCOW IN MY SIGHTS!

BY BOBBY CHARLTON

MY personal list of honours stretches across a long career of top flight football with my club, Manchester United, and with England.

But one of the greatest honours that ever came my way concerned neither United nor England; it didn't earn me a cap, a cup or any sort of trophy but, nevertheless, it gave me as great a thrill as I have ever had in soccer.

It was an invitation from my old friend and rival Lev Yashin, the Russian goalkeeper, who graced the world's grounds with his agility and superb mastery of his own job.

Yashin asked me to play in a world eleven against his side, Moscow Dynamo, in the Russian capital. It was to be his final appearance as a player in the Lenin stadium with a full-house of more than 100,000 Russian spectators.

George Best, Bobby Moore and Gordon Banks had been invited, too, but for various reasons they couldn't make it. And I was to be the lone representative from Britain.

The invitation had been sent to the FA by the Russian football federation and Sir Matt Busby thought it would be a good idea for me to represent United and the British Isles in Moscow and he readily agreed that I should go.

United were to be on tour in Austria and I had somehow to sandwich the trip to Russia in between two games that my own club was playing. In fact, it left me only one and a half days in Moscow. The trip, as you can see, had to be brief with no time for sightseeing.

Once before I had been to Moscow, and the fabulous Lenin stadium, to play for England against Russia ten years ago, in 1961.

And, in a long span of matches against the Russians, I had never managed to get the ball past Yashin. He always seemed to pull out something extra special against me.

Once or twice I had almost been throwing my hands high to celebrate a goal when the tall, angular Russian had telescoped himself into an impossible save.

I wondered on the long flight from Vienna, where United were playing on tour, to Moscow if I could get one past him at this point of his career. . .

Yashin is one of the most respected men in soccer, he had endeared himself to fans all over the world with his sportsmanship and, of course,

95

his incredible skills. I don't suppose anybody who saw him, for instance, in Stanley Matthews' benefit at Stoke would forget the unbelievable reflex saves he pulled off.

Manchester United's feeling about Yashin's reputation were such that they footed the bill for my trip to Moscow. And I was only too pleased, and proud, too, to be asked to go.

I had met Yashin socially on only one or two occasions and I found him a charming man. We had shared a bottle of vodka a couple of times. Once he and his teammate, the great Russian player, Voronin, slipped their watchful guards to bring a bottle to my hotel bedroom for a modest booze-up.

The cold war was at its lowest ebb and the Russians were not really supposed to mix with outsiders—but this, for me, showed how a great game like football can break down even political barriers. Footballers the world over are basically the same; they have only the interests of the game at heart.

In the secrecy of my room we talked, with sign language and with a little smattering of English from Yashin, only about soccer. He and Voronin, a really splendid half-back who would have been a top man in any team, were floored when we told them what sort of money we could earn.

Their wages then were something like £30 a month! I don't suppose they are much more now.

It was with this sort of background friendship, extended at meetings in Portugal, Rome and in London and Mexico, that I felt it would be a bad let down for him if I couldn't make it for my appointment in Moscow.

United played in Klagenfurt, Austria, in July 1971, and moved on to Vienna for another game—and that's where I left them.

A visa had been rushed through for me; United gave me my air ticket and off I went to join some of the world's finest players who were all only too pleased to give up their spare time to take part in this prestige match.

Gerd Muller and Schulz arrived from Germany: Pena came from Mexico, Dumitrache, from Rumania; Mazurkiewicz, the goalkeeper

Gordon Banks . . . he missed it.

from Uruguay; Meszoly, from Hungary; Dragan Dzajic, from Belgrade, all to play in the special white commemorative shirts bearing the Yashin memorial crest. It was a great side.

We hardly knew each other's names, we hadn't trained together, but with players like that you don't have to worry about such trifles. It all happened off the cuff!

We were told simply to go out and enjoy ourselves—and put on a treat. But it turned into a full-scale match in the fullest sense of the word.

96

The Moscow Dynamo team took it deadly seriously and tore into us, they really wanted to win and they tried like mad. They went ahead 2—0—but we hit back and made it 2—2 in a hard fought game.

I thought I'd scored the winner when I managed to get a fair crack at Yashin—but, once again, he foiled me with a super save.

Just like scoring against Gordon Banks getting one against Yashin was a major achievement and something to boast about; I don't, unfortunately, have the satisfaction of having done it. He was well past 40 years of age when he played in this match—but he was as lively as ever.

I had a farewell glass of vodka with him and his wife before I left to resume my tour with United in Vienna, a promise he had kept with me to share another bottle.

Even as my taxi was skirting the edge of the Red Square, passing the Bolshoi theatre, on its way to the airport I remember thinking that we would never see the like of the player again.

And, of course, wondering if we would ever meet up again. It could be that Manchester United will be matched against the club he coaches, Moscow Dynamo, in one of Europe's top contests.

I hope so. For both our sakes.

Neil Ramsbottom untangles his goal.

97

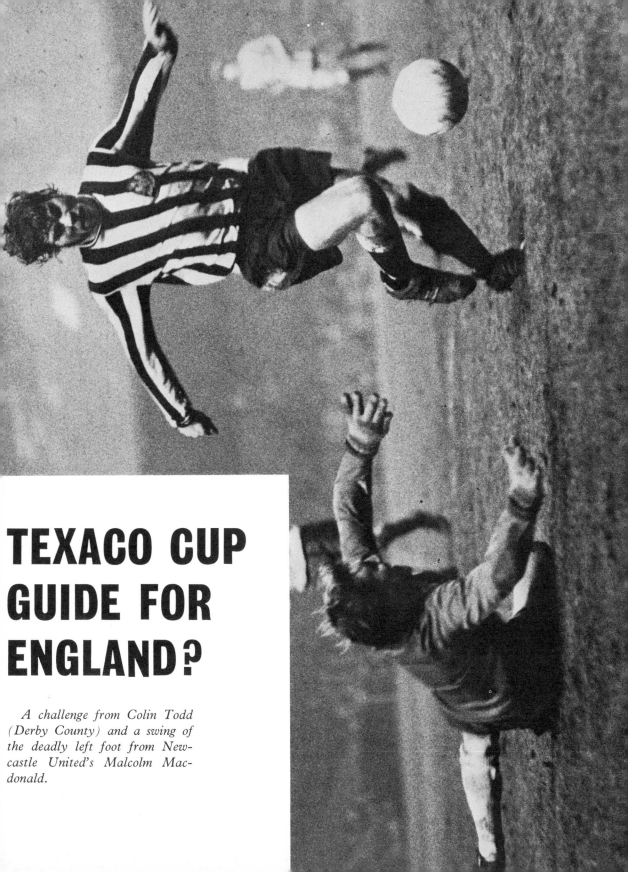

TEXACO CUP GUIDE FOR ENGLAND?

A challenge from Colin Todd (Derby County) and a swing of the deadly left foot from Newcastle United's Malcolm Macdonald.

BATTLE ROYLE!

Mud-stained Joe Royle, the Everton leader, battles it out (left) against Tottenham Hotspur and on the right against another of the League's top sides, Derby County.

From Burnley to big-time

BY RALPH COATES

O N reflection I could not have done better than join Tottenham when I left Burnley at the end of last season. I though so at the time but now, after my first year at White Hart Lane, I am convinced of it.

There are several reasons, some less obvious than others. Add them all together and my move to London was a case of a square peg going into a square hole. Everything fitted. No regrets for me—and I hope none on Tottenham's side.

On the face of it the move to Tottenham looked ideal. But nothing is predictable in soccer. Many players have found it hard to settle into new surroundings.

I had always been content at Burnley. There was never a day I was not happy at the club. They treated me well and gave me my big break in football. I will always be thankful to them and hold a deep affection for the club and the people connected with it.

Every player must be ambitious. And it was my ambition, and that alone, which made me glad to be leaving Turf Moor. When we failed to avoid relegation I realised I would damage my chances of achieving my ambitions by staying with the club in the Second Division.

A footballer's life is a short one, probably averaging about 15 years. So much can depend on having the right breaks. Being at the right place at the right time. I did not doubt—nor do I now—

Martin Chivers and Alan Gilzean.

A strong challenge from Colin Waldron of Burnley (right).

that Burnley would be a soccer power again but not in the immediate future. And I wanted both club and personal success before it was too late.

My dreams were those of every professional player. A Wembley Cup Final, a championship medal and so on. And on a more personal level a place in the England team.

I had been to Mexico with the England party for the 1970 World Cup. It was a great experience. I was disappointed to be left out of the final squad of 22 but I nursed hopes—and still do—of playing a part in the next competition in Munich in 1974.

I heard that a lot of big clubs were interested in me—both United and City at Manchester, Leeds and Arsenal among them. But it was Tottenham who stepped in.

My thoughts were far from a transfer when I was mowing my lawn at home one day and was suddenly told Tottenham had agreed terms with Burnley. A few hours later I had signed for them.

It was all very hush-hush. I was taken to a Staffordshire hotel to meet Tottenham manager Bill Nicholson but when we arrived the place was so crowded we moved into the car park. In the back of a car, belonging to Burnley manager Jimmy Adamson, I put my name on the dotted line.

I often feel that my performance for England against Greece just before had clinched the transfer—all FIFTEEN MINUTES of it. I was called on as substitute and was determined to make the most of a brief appearance. I knew I did well. I got a lot of the ball and everything went right for me. Bill Nicholson could well have made his final decision on seeing me that night.

Did that transfer fee of around £190,000 worry me? That was the question I was continually asked after going to Tottenham.

I can honestly say it has not. After all, I played no part in putting a valuation on myself. That was between the two managers. And with Alan Ball going to North London neighbours Arsenal for £220,000 my fee no longer looks so enormous.

But here is one reason why Tottenham suited me. With so many expensive players—Martin

104

Martin Peters.

Peters at £200,000 and Martin Chivers at £120,000 for example—my fee did not have as much impact as it might at another club.

If I had gone to a club who had made few big-money signings I would have stuck out like a sore thumb. There would have been a lot more pressure on me. Supporters might have expected miracles.

At Tottenham I also knew I would be among some of the country's best players. I had to benefit from it. We had a lot of talent at Burnley but perhaps what we lacked was experience. This was not the case at Tottenham. So many of the players had a background of football at the highest sphere both at domestic, European and international grade.

Tottenham were also one of the best clubs in the First Division and as such always challenged for the top honours.

I must admit I was nervous about making my home debut. The way some of the lads spoke about the Tottenham supporters I had visions of them turning up with shotguns. Seriously though I knew that in the past they had sometimes been slow to accept newcomers.

Alan Mullery and Martin Chivers were given a rough ride at first. But then Alan had to take over from Dave Mackay, the almost legendary Scot, and Martin from Jimmy Greaves, who was worshipped by the fans. My case was a little different. I was not following in anyone's footsteps.

We played at Wolves on the opening day of the season and did well to draw 2–2. I remember wishing that it had been at home so that debut would have been behind me. But I need not have worried because a few days later in a mid-week match with Newcastle the Tottenham supporters gave me a marvellous welcome.

I started off at Tottenham playing as a more orthodox winger instead of operating in midfield. It was difficult to adjust at first. I used to have the run of the park at Burnley. I felt restricted having to stay up field and wide on the flanks. But I did my best.

I must admit I was happier when switched

back to midfield later on. I have always loved being continually involved in everything. It was also easier to prove effective when supported by men like Martin Peters and young Steve Perryman.

I soon had another new experience and not a happy one. I was put out of action for about six weeks with a hamstring injury. I would hate to have to go through that torment again.

It came at a time when I really felt I was building up a good understanding with my new team-mates and clicking into top gear myself. Then in a League Cup match at Torquay I received this injury.

I thought I would soon be back. Throughout my career I had been lucky with injuries. I was called a quick healer. One who was able to shrug off knocks and strains quickly. But not this one.

Tottenham were concerned that I did not push myself too hard. They realised that if I had come back too soon when not completely 100 per cent fit I ran the risk of breaking down again and missing even more matches.

So it was a gradual process. It was a terrible time. I became very depressed on occasions. Some days the leg seemed fine but then on others it did not feel any better. I kept getting pain when

Coates . . . and England men.

105

I really went into a full-out sprint or stretched the leg.

But the nightmare finally came to an end. I was back in the side and my misery was a thing of the past. When Alan Mullery had to drop out of the team with a stomach complaint for such a long time I knew the agony he was going through.

One aspect of my own play I have tried to develop since going to Tottenham has been putting more emphasis on getting into good positions in front of goal.

At Burnley I was never really concerned with scoring goals or looking for the space to get into the role of finisher. But at Tottenham I have found that more and more chances were coming my way.

I suppose it has to do with the quality of the players around me. You do not have to worry whether certain men will be doing their jobs—you know they will. Consequently, I have more scope and freedom to move forward when possible.

I have always been a creator of goals but from now on I want to help with the finished product.

I am positive that Tottenham will be sharing many of the top honours in the next few years. Just look at the talent at the club.

In Martin Chivers we have the most effective striker in the business; in midfield the subtle skills of Martin Peters; at the back the dominating figure of Mike England and goalkeeper Pat Jennings must rank second only to Gordon Banks.

Yes, the future is a bright one. And I want to be very much a part of that Tottenham success story.

John O'Hare, Derby County and Scotland.

RACE FOR CAPS

Colin Todd (Derby County) yet to be capped for England and Tony Green (Newcastle United) already an international for Scotland.

Red choir…

Blue ballet...

RISE AND FALL OF THE STARS

goes Arsenal's George Graham for a header
ft) and, above, down go Liverpool centre half
rry Lloyd and Denis Law of Manchester
ited.

Here is the face of a man who does not know fear

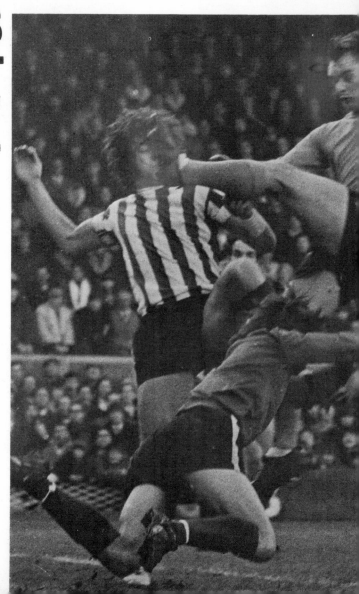

Are goalkeepers really crazy? They are certainly brave as Brentford's Gordon Phillips shows in this piece of action as he fearlessly plunges out to save. And (top right) that's how the man behind the save really looks.

*. . . and this man doesn't
need to watch the ball*

GLAZIER'S BALL

It's all feet and arms but, as pretty often, it's the keeper who gets there first. And this time it's

MAINE ROAD MINUET

. . . and the "dancers" taking part are John Talbut of West Bromwich Albion, and Manchester City's Mike Summerbee.

I want Europe to tremble . .

BY FRANK O'FARRELL

WHEN you have charge of the tiller of a club like Manchester United you can expect that at times you will be steering a bumpy voyage to success.

That fact came home to me when the season ran from 1971 and into 1972 and we hit a stormy passage.

We drifted from a five point lead down to four or five places below the new leaders, our cross-city rivals Manchester City.

And, with the loss of status a lot of our confidence seemed to sink, too. We struggled and fought but achieved only fading form which culminated in that awful and awesome leathering handed out by Leeds United. Five–one we went down to turn 1972, up to then without a win for us, into an absolute disaster.

At the time of writing I don't know where we will finish up in the league—but I must say by the end of the season I will be a much wiser manager.

Ironically, I will have learned more out of defeat than I would have done had Manchester United gone on winning week after week.

One discovers true character in the face of adversity; it's a time when people, and footballers, too, show the stuff they are made of.

If there are any fighting qualities they obviously show more starkly when the chips are down and this, for me, was just as important as learning from the buoyancy of success.

Every player at Manchester United is a target for every other professional's ire in soccer; they all want to beat us, our reputation is such, and our

Nobby Stiles.

Man in the middle of the mobbing—George Best after scoring against Huddersfield Town.

pride is such, that all the other clubs naturally want to give us a beating.

The fans at Old Trafford are great in number and demanding as they have a right to be; they want success, Manchester United need it and we are all aiming for it.

But the howl that went up when we were shaken off our winning way showed me that sometimes fans can be puzzling.

The clamour was enormous; I was in the hot seat, the target for everybody's abuse when things began to go awry.

The great shout was for me to sign somebody, anybody, quick. And, believe me, I was certainly aware of the pressures of managership during this period.

Steve James.

118

But if these people thought that the only time I was looking for new players was when the crisis hit the club they are very much mistaken.

Almost from my first weeks at the club I was nosing into the transfer market hunting out the sort of players I thought United might need; it was uppermost in my mind to strengthen the club right from the beginning of my time there.

I suppose I realised then that the job of being the boss of the world's most famous and respected team was not all roses. And, I admit, I felt frustrated that I simply could not get the men I wanted and had to watch the lead skip from us unarrested in its downward run.

But the facts behind the scenes should be simple to appreciate—the players just were not available. I went for men I knew would be great for us, but they were not for transfer.

There was some difficult and long drawn out bartering, as there always is in any transfer, but the result always seemed to be the same: NO SALE.

Manchester United is a wealthy club and I was given a free hand to spend all the money I needed, around £500,000, to build up the force I fancied. But money in the bank is no use, players are what you need. And that view was shared by managers of other clubs. . . . In the end I succeeded and managed to buy two magnificent young players, Martin Buchan, from Aberdeen, and Ian Moore, from Forest.

They didn't want cash in the bank, they wanted players, too, to replace the ones they would be selling. And what you get is a lot of managers all going round in the transfer circle trying to fill gaps with no players to fill them.

The difficulty of picking up a great young player, getting him into the team quickly, is a process that is so rare as to be unfeasible. The answer is a ready-made star, not a raw youngster, who can slot in quickly and effectively. We have plenty of up and coming young ones in the reserve and "A" teams—but they were not ready or capable of helping us in the dilemma we suffered early in 1972.

There is also a mistaken belief that the "old

Eusebio in action.

(By ALEXANDRE BAPTISTA)
(Sporting Lisbon and Portugal)

I AM very pleased to write about Bobby. And I say it is easy and difficult to play against him. It is difficult because he is one of the best players in the world, easy because you have only to worry about playing football.

I know people compare him with Pele and Eusebio but you cannot really compare them: Bobby plays in the middle of the field where he is among the best and Eusebio and Pele play in the area.

When you reach such a high standard of playing you do not need to play rough, and if anyone play as Bobby do who would think to hit the man not the ball?

He is very popular in Portugal and what I admire most in his play is this: he releases or stays with the ball only when he must.

He is a fine man, a good opposition and very much admired all over the world.

SOCCER AS WE SEE IT

WIM VAN HANEGEM, the man who makes Feyenoord and Holland tick, tells how he made it to the top when he thought he was a failure.

OF all the well-known soccer players in Europe I am probably the one who started his big-time career last of all.

I am 28 now—but I did not start to move in important football circles until 12 years ago. That is when I was discovered as a youth with some talent for the game.

I tried two teams in my hometown of Utrecht, Holland, but I was not accepted. First I went to Elinkwijk and was told I was not good enough.

Then, a bit chastened, I transferred myself to the other team in the town, DOS, a famous Dutch side with a good turnover in young talent.

But they told me I had to come back a few days later and play in a trial match. I did not like the idea of that and, being a stubborn young fellow, even at 16, I refused to go back for the run-out.

I thought my career had ended even before it had begun. A failure at sixteen!

I did not get much chance to play soccer in those days. My friends were always playing, sometimes in the streets, but many of them did not like me joining in their games because I was always passing remarks about them during the matches.

And, in fact, they all came to call me "The Grumbler"—a name and a reputation that has stuck with me all these years.

Nowadays you may see me in a game muttering to myself; but it is more of a habit than anything else, I don't mean anything bad by it. It probably looks bad from the terraces. But most of the remarks I make on the pitch are directed at myself—nobody else.

I am seldom happy with my own play, rarely content about the way I have done something and certainly always anxious to improve.

I try to remember the things I do wrong so I may analyse them afterwards and make sure I do not do it wrong again.

When I was a brash teenager, with a longing to play soccer, I was jealous of my pals because most of them were turning out for Velox, the very excellent third team in Utrecht.

I was so bored with my inactivity, but still so anxious to be in the atmosphere of soccer, that I used to go and stand behind the goals at Velox training sessions and kick the ball back when it went wide or came near me.

I always hit it with my left foot, I was never able to hit a good ball with my right. I believe, anyway, like Bobby Charlton that you can be a good player, an excellent one, without having to use both feet.

The club trainer, Daan van Beek, had watched me whacking the ball back onto the pitch and seemed impressed enough with my kicking to invite me to join the club! What a switch! Everything seemed to go at express speed after that.

In two years, after working my way with a little more patience, through the Junior sides, I became a regular member of the first team and was given the job of schemer in the side.

I do not think I was a very good player then, I was overweight for one thing, much heavier than I am now, and I always used to keep the ball in my possession. I was allowed to do it then—but now, no.

I was a hell-raiser, too, and rather turbulent. Once, because of my stormy character, I was suspended for 12 weeks. There was, I think, a certain amount of justification in the action that had me sent off; I laid out an apponent who had bitten me on my back.

A year later I was suspended again. This time because of a joke I played on a referee. He had given a free kick to the opposition and when I passed the ball to him I put my foot under it and gave it so much back-spin that, as he bent to pick it up, it bounced back to me.

He was terribly angry and demanded my name.

When I answered: "Willem", he thought I was taking the mickey. He was called Willem, too, and he thought, for some reason, I was making a fool of him. I was reported—and suspended.

I still have my problems with refs—but I am a much wiser man these days. But I have greater problems with opponents.

I am physically exceptionally strong and when I have the ball it is difficult for anybody to get it off me; it irritates defenders to distraction. And when I play the ball between their legs they get even more angry.

It gives me a chance to gain some valuable space and some yards advantage, I need this because I am hardly the quickest player around. I know I am so slow that some fans have nicknamed me "The Turtle".

I seemed to be born to collect nicknames. For I have another one—"The Curved One". And it's nothing to do with the way I am built. It is because when I make a pass I always seem to curve it and can hardly kick a ball in a straight line.

I am such a one-legged player that I have to curve the ball to make up for the uselessness of my right foot. My right foot is so weak that, in all my career, I have never scored a goal with it.

Once I had a bet that I could knock one in with my right foot—but, even two yards from goal, I managed to hit the ball sky-high over the top.

The one and only time I managed to hit the ball nicely with my right a defender stopped the ball with his hands on the line. I'll celebrate when I do score with my "swinger" leg.

I prefer to 'make' the goals, I have carried on my style as a schemer, but with one or two breaks in other positions in between times.

They were great years, and enjoyable, too, at Xerxes/DHC and I learned a lot under their trainer, Kurt Linder, one of the finest in Holland.

When the team was disbanded because of lack of money I should have gone to Eindhoven but the fee asked was too high and they would not pay so much.

Ajax, the great European Dutchmen, did not want me either. Their trainer thought I was too slow and did not make a bid.

Instead I went to my favourite team, Feyenoord, the side I wanted to play for above all others. It would have been great at Ajax, playing with Johan Cruyff and Piet Keizer, two really fabulous footballers, but Feyenoord made the offer and that's where I went.

Feyenoord were a big-time team and ambitious for success. And, under Ernst Happel, we had a really grand time. He led us to the European Cup in his first year with the club.

That, without any doubt, was the highlight of my career. And I shall never forget it.

Winning, to me, is all important. I don't mean a win at any costs, I don't have a mean streak in me but I do have a tremendous will to win at anything I attempt.

That is why I battle for the ball in every game: I am a determined player, but not dirty. I will chase a man all over the pitch in order to get the ball from him. If I lose the ball I harry the man who robbed me until I get it back again. That's the way the game has to be contested.

I suppose I am a hard player, but I like to think that I am fair. I hate to see how men like Cruyff and Keizer are dealt with by some opponents.

Last season led Feyenoord into black times in Europe—we were the shock knock-out side of the European Cup when we were dismissed by a little known Rumanian team, Arad.

We could not believe it—there had never been such a shock for us. But, a year later, we were the Dutch champions again and once more back into Europe.

I do not think our team is as strong as it has been in the past, not as strong, for instance, as the one that beat Celtic 2–1 in the European Cup final two years ago, but we still want to show that we are one of the finest sides in Europe.

We went back to Rumania looking for some sort of revenge for that defeat by Arad—and we got it by beating Dynamo Bucharest 3–0 on their own ground.

WORLD STRIKERS

Florian Albert (Hungary).

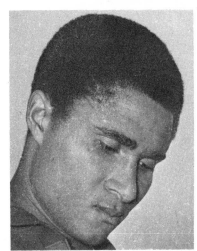

Eusebio (Portugal).

Uwe Seeler (W. Germany).

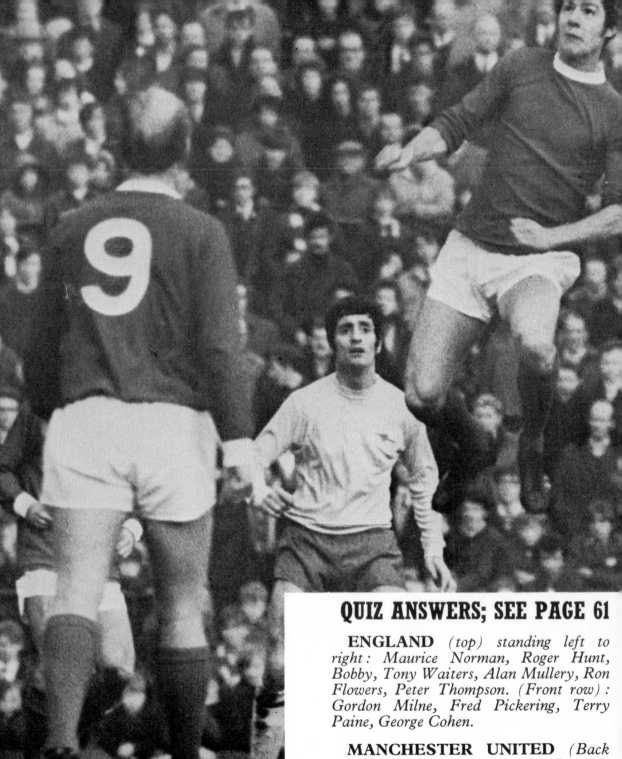

Leaping action from Brian Kidd.

QUIZ ANSWERS; SEE PAGE 61

ENGLAND *(top) standing left to right:* Maurice Norman, Roger Hunt, Bobby, Tony Waiters, Alan Mullery, Ron Flowers, Peter Thompson. *(Front row):* Gordon Milne, Fred Pickering, Terry Paine, George Cohen.

MANCHESTER UNITED *(Back row):* Foulkes, Aston, Rimmer, Stepney, Gowling, Herd. *(Middle row):* Sadler, Dunne, Brennan, Crerand, Best, Burns, trainer Crompton. *(Front row):* Ryan, Stiles, Law, Sir Matt Busby, Bobby, Kidd, and Fitzpatrick.

Jack Charlton . . . a goal in his 600th game.

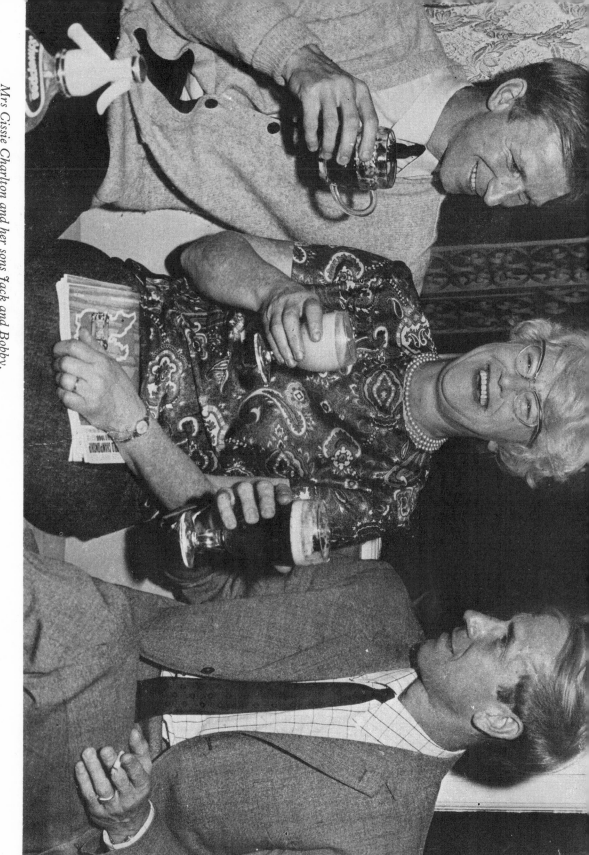

Mrs Cissie Charlton and her sons Jack and Bobby.